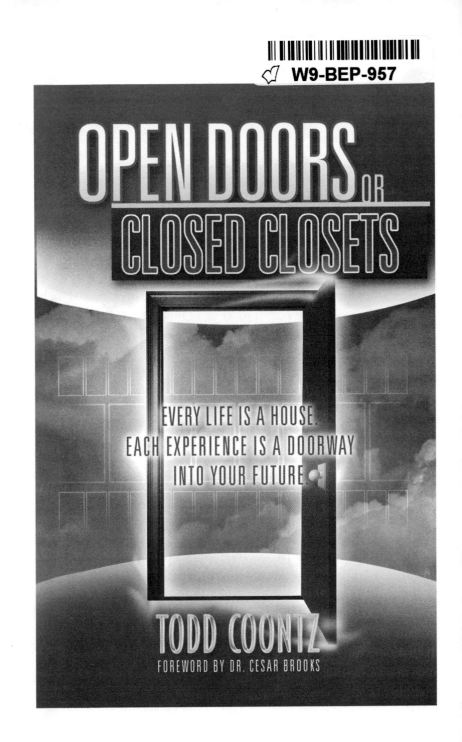

OPEN DOORS OR CLOSED CLOSETS

EVERY LIFE IS A HOUSE.
EACH EXPERIENCE IS A DOORWAY
INTO YOUR FUTURE.

TODD COONTZ

FOREWORD BY DR. CESAR BROOKS

Open Doors or Closed Closets: Every Life Is A House. Each Experience Is A Doorway Into Your Future.

ISBN 1-931600-23-6

ROCKWEALTH MINISTRIES
P.O. Box 6177
Aiken, South Carolina 29804-6177

Printed in the United States of America.

Editorial Content – Deborah Murdock Johnson
Book Cover Design – Bryant Design
Printed By – Faith Printing, Inc.

~*Foreword*~

Everyone loves a "Rags-to-Riches" story!

For over ten years as Todd Coontz's pastor, I have had the distinct and unique pleasure of watching his *journey* unfold before my very eyes. His quest for wisdom has transformed his meager beginnings to this season of Godly abundance, and yet Todd remains teachable; humble, and loyal to his Church.

Todd Coontz documents desire coupled with information with a constant pursuit for excellence will move anyone's life forward as it has for him. I know everyone reading this book will find it both informational and inspirational. If you are like me you'll probably have your favorite chapter, my personal favorite — *"Don't Repo My Car."* This chapter chronicles Todd's true-to-life success story and reveals to the reader, very specific *Wisdom Principles* anyone can follow.

Todd brings a unique perspective as a successful business-man. He has diligently applied these Godly principles, and is now enjoying a season of God's blessings and abundance. Because of his success in business and faithfulness in pursuing God for over 26 years uniquely qualifies him to speak to us with authority on these important principles.

My prayer is that every person who reads this book will allow the wisdom documented in every chapter to transform their heart and mind, and thrust them into a new season of Godly achievement.

Advancing His Kingdom,
Pastor Cesar A. Brooks

~Dedication~

I dedicate this book to my first mentor and father in the Lord —
Rev. Bud Marshall.

For the first ten years of my walk with Christ, he tirelessly spent
endless hours *teaching* me the laws of God. Although, I didn't always want to follow his instructions because of my stubborness, he
still remained patient with me.

Through his love and wisdom God used him to lay a foundation
in my life which has enabled me to build a successful life. His *obedience* to the call of God and faithfulness to that call afforded me the
opportunity to also respond to God's call on my life.

Thank-you Bud for loving me, and for answering the call of God
to preach this gospel faithfully. Most of all, thank-you for introduc-
ing me to my best friend — Jesus.

Your Spiritual Son,

Todd Coontz

~ *Special Thanks* ~

Dove Broadcasting, Inc. — Jimmy & Joanne Thompson
First Family Church of Augusta — Pastor Cesar & Sherry Brooks
Lamb Broadcasting, Inc. — Charles & Lela Reed
Watchmen Broadcasting, Inc. — Russell & Dorothy Spaulding
Talbott Funeral Home, Inc. — Michael & Charlene Talbott

Anastacio & Eugenia Arenivas	Chris B. Emerson
Billy & June Brazell	Deborah Evans
Daniel Brazell	Galen & Paulette Haffner
Mark & Christina Brazell	Kenneth & Jeanie Lamb
John & Ruby Brown	Richard Lento
Ellen Catlet	Marcia McCormick
Carolyn Davis	Evelyne Samuel
Pushpa Dewan	Shirley Smith
Janie Dixon	

~Introduction~

Remember the first time you made a decision to accept Christ as your Savior? It felt as though a *ton* had been lifted off of your back. It left you with a feeling of *relief.* You knew that you had been given another chance on life. *This time you weren't going to blow it!* Excitement filled your heart and you couldn't wait to share with others this newfound joy! That decision started you on a new journey with a fresh start on life.

It wasn't very long after you started your journey with God that you discovered even though your *spirit man* became regenerated, your flesh wasn't always willing to cooperate. A *struggle* between the spirit man and the flesh existed. Too often you found yourself beaten, bruised, and defeated. Although you read books on how to conquer the flesh and gain victory over the devil, you still found yourself struggling. Many times faced with life's disappointments and even tragedy, your *faith* and *zeal* of becoming something great for God started to diminish. *Dreams* that once flourished with life and enthusiasm withered and died! Those great aspirations you once possessed about accomplishing something great for Him seemed all but a fading memory. Your *love* for God did not grow dim; however, your hope of being a great warrior for God was lost under years of defeat, hurt, and pain.

I still believe the words of Jesus... *"The works that I do ye shall do; and even greater works because I go to my Father and will send you back another Comforter...."* **Open Doors or Closed Closets** has been birthed through times of defeat, hurt, and pain. Every experience has brought a new *challenge*. Each encounter with hurt gave God an opportunity to heal and reveal His compassion to me. In spite of every brush with pain, and through every struggle coming from a variety of circumstances, God always used each experience to shape, mold, and develop me into His image, allowing these experiences to become a *doorway* into my future!

I began writing this book in 1995. This book has been laying in my study waiting to be completed for over seven years now. The Holy Spirit knew He still had some work to do in me before I could finish it. Today, July 12, 2002, I'm now completing the final chapters. He is still not through with me yet; however, tremendous growth has taken place in my life. Find a quiet place to read. My prayer is that you would allow the Holy Spirit to bring healing into your life. He will *rekindle* your dreams! He will *rebirth* the hope you once had of becoming a person of greatness! He will *empower* you to do the greater works! Open every closet door to Him, and allow Him to bring restoration and healing. When you are willing to open each *closed* closet door perhaps filled with pain, hurt, disappointments, and even character flaws...He can help you to step into your future. **Every Life Is A House. Each Experience Is A Doorway Into Your Future!**

~Todd Coontz~

~*Table of Contents*~

Foreword
Dedication
Introduction

Dreams Do Come True

"And Joseph dreamed a dream, and he told it to his brethren: and they hated him yet the more."

Genesis 37:5

CHAPTER 1

*T*oday my life is much different than I dreamed possible. I can testify to you of God's goodness and that dreams do come true. As I begin to write this first chapter I'm almost overwhelmed by the things that God has done for me. Really, I'm having difficulty narrowing down where I should start. So, I've concluded that like all success stories people like to hear where you are today first, then they want to learn more about the journey that carried you to success. Why should I break the tradition?

Today, I'm the owner of a business called, *Coontz Investments & Insurance, Inc.* I've been successfully helping people plan financially for over a decade now. People have entrusted with me their investments which easily equals millions of dollars. I have been married to my wife, Dana for over 10 years, and together we're raising our son, Landon who will soon turn nine-years-old. Recently, we built another new home in the estate section of the city, where homes sell for upwards of a million dollars. I started my second company about a year ago called, *RockWealth Ministries* where I travel throughout the country teaching people how to qualify, receive, and manage wealth. Through the media of television, radio, and books — I teach God's people the message of prosperity based on Biblical principles. I'm also a private pilot and regularly fly myself to my speaking engagements. I am only 36 years old and God has helped me achieve incredible success, both spiritually and financially. Nearly every dream I've ever had has been fulfilled. In fact, God rebirthed in me more dreams to accomplish with my life. Please...I don't want to leave you with the impression that I'm bragging or boasting about what I have and have done — *I'm not.*

What I want you to gain from this is that if God can do this for me, then He can certainly do it for you! My life has not always been so successful — really just the opposite would apply. As you will soon see from an early age I was faced with some incredible challenges, and many told me that I would never amount to anything. Yet, God saw something in me that the eye's of others failed to recognize. I want to take you on a journey through these written pages that took place over 26 years ago in an old country Church. As I chronicle my life and share with you very intimate happenings, my prayer is that each *experience* will help you to become more of what God wants you to be. Dreams do come true!

We find in Genesis a young man who started early in his life dreaming. He learned early the importance of dreaming, and more importantly about God-given dreams. I believe in the importance of dreams. *I believe that it's as important to dream as it is to breathe.* You can't live without breathing; however, if you have lost your dreams then your future will suffocate! What are dreams? Dreams are *visions* in your minds. Dreams are *expectations* of the great things you will do. Dreams are your *reason* for getting up each morning. Dreams are your *hope* for a better life. Dreams give you substance of *life* by giving you the assurance that you can make a difference. Dreams are *seeds* waiting to be planted, watered, and fertilized so they can give you a bountiful harvest! They are planted by God in those who have a *hunger* to do something extraordinary. They are watered by *action* coupled with the pursuit of their destiny. They are fertilized with a burning *desire* to be accomplished. *Dreams Are Goals With A Deadline!*

God does have a plan for your life. The *tools* He uses to carry out these plans are dreams. His plan is an overview of His *purpose* for your life. *Dreams are like pieces to a puzzle:* He uses each dream to fit neatly together to fulfill His overall plan. As His plans unfold so do the *dreams* He has purposed for your life. I believe that nothing is by coincidence or chance. God has a way of fulfilling every dream He places in your heart. When you make a decision to pursue your dreams, God will make them possible according to *Jeremiah 32:27: "Behold, I am the Lord, the God of all flesh: is there any thing too hard for me?"* So let's dream big dreams because He is a big God!

I want to discuss with you the *three stages* dreams go through starting with germination to the final stages of maturity. I believe that God is *calling* forth His people in these last days to dream... and to dream big! Everybody who has been born again *qualifies* for the fulfillment of their dreams. Get ready, because God is breathing *life* back into the dreams of your past, present, and future!

STAGE # 1...THE BIRTH OF A DREAM

There has been much discussion in the past several years about the issue of abortion. Is it murder? This controversy is centered around the question "When does life really begin?" Some believe that life begins outside of the mother's womb, while others say that life starts at conception. Yet, there are still those who candidly admit that it really doesn't matter, because it is the mother's right to choose. *I believe that life begins at conception!* When the sperm unites with the female egg life starts. It is God who gives life! *Genesis 2:7 says, "And the Lord God formed man of the dust of the ground, and breathed into his nostrils the breath of life; and man became a living soul."* God also breathes life into every good dream. *"Every good gift and every perfect gift is from above, and cometh down from the Father of lights, with whom is no variableness, neither shadow of turning" (James 1:17).* Don't forget... it is God who is the giver of your dreams!

All of us have had dreams. Some of them first appeared as a child, while others were birthed during adulthood. What are your dreams today? Do dreams even come true? *Yes, they do!* Recently, my parents had the opportunity to come and visit us; we don't get to see them much because they live in another state. But when we do get to see them we enjoy the time we spend with them. My father and I were having lunch one day when the subject of his military days came up. He was in the Navy — he retired with 20 years of service. He was telling me about a story concerning being transferred from one location to another while he was in the Navy. I want to share this story with you because I believe it illustrates the general attitude concerning people and their belief system about dreams and whether they come true. He explained to me that after someone had finished their assignment, the Navy would sometimes require you to move to another state where you would be given your next assignment. The Navy really didn't give you any choice...you would be required to move somewhere else to begin another assignment. The Navy would give to you what they called *"dream sheets"* and on them would be a list of possible places to go. You would then have the opportunity to choose where you wanted to live for your next assignment. My father said, *"It was very rare to ever get what you asked for."* In fact, he told me that over the twenty years he spent in the Navy, after filling out many *"dream sheets"* he could not remember the Navy ever granting his request. I was *surprised* to hear this! You might have faced something similar in your life. Disappointment may be the only result you've received after believing in your dreams. You may think that dreams really do not come true. At best you may believe that if they do come true, they will probably come true for somebody else. *There Is Hope For Your Dreams!* I want to help you *rekindle* your desire to dream!

Let's start by defining what dreams are. Dreams are *desires* that you have. They are *things* that you want to achieve. They can be *visions* of greatness. They are *ideas*. Dreams are those things that bring you the most excitement! Everybody needs to feel like they have achieved something great with their life. You need to feel like you are giving to others and your life is making a difference. *When You Stop Producing, You Have The Tendency To Become Lonely And Lazy!* Your reason for living diminishes and all enthusiasm is choked out from your being. God plants these dreams in you so that you will have something to strive for. In you resides the nature of God. His very nature demands *increase* and *productivity!* He created you to be productive which results in fulfillment. After all, if laziness was fulfilling then nothing would ever get accomplished. God is pleased when you accomplish your dreams. It perhaps may be the highest form of our faith...to set out and fulfill the impossible! *God Has An Incredible Desire To Be Believed!* When your dreams are fulfilled it reminds the devil of everything he lost because of his rebellion. *It Throws...Faith...Back Into His Face!*

When God gives you a dream He will also give you the necessary *gifts* to fulfill your dreams according to *Romans 12:6: "Having then gifts differing according to the grace that is given to us, whether prophecy, let us prophesy according to the proportion of faith." 1 Corinthians 12:4: "Now there are diversities of gifts, but the same Spirit."* If you continue to read this chapter it names many gifts and sums them all up in *verse 11: "But all these worketh that one and the selfsame Spirit, dividing to every man severally [many] as he will."* God is the giver of your dreams and He also gives you the gifts necessary to bring them to pass. Don't live in the *tomb* of past failures! Believe God to fulfill every dream you have! Past failures will not disqualify you from your dreams! *Romans 11:29 declares, "For the gifts and calling of God are without repentance."* The Greek word here translated repentance in this verse means *"irrevocable."* I like the way John L. Mason in his book called *An Enemy Called Average* sums this up. He says, "God cannot take away His gifts and calling in your life. Even if you've never done anything with them, even if you've failed time and time again, God's gifts and calling are still resident in you."

God has blessed me with the ability to *dream* big. I have seen many of my dreams come to pass during my life. As I fulfill each of them, God plants another dream in my heart so I can use my faith to bring glory to Him. He never gives to us at once *all* of our lifetime dreams. We would probably faint! So He gives them by measure...over time...one piece at a time. Let me share with you a dream of mine that recently took place. When I was about 12 years old, I had a friend named Chuckie. His parents had a grandfather clock in the foyer of their house. I remember hearing it chime every time I stayed overnight with him; it was very pleasant and I really enjoyed listening to it. Ever since that time I have always envisioned my home having one. Recently, my wife and I purchased a Howard Miller grand-father clock. God reminded me one day as I enjoyed its chimes that He had fulfilled yet another dream of mine. I inscribed on a brass plate in the inside door of the clock the word "DREAM" to remind me that God not only gives us dreams, but He also fulfills them. *So Dream Big Dreams Because He Is A Big God!*

STAGE # 2...STEWARDSHIP OF A DREAM

Gifts and talents are really God's deposits in your personal accounts, and you determine the interest on them. The greater the amount of interest and attention you give to them, the greater the value becomes. *God's gifts are never loans; they are always deposits!* God expects from you the multiplication of every talent and gift He gives you. It's your responsibility to bring Him a good return and to grow your talents so dividends can be paid. The dividends are the *recognition* that God provided the talents and gifts. Your *talents* and *gifts* are tools used to fulfill God's dreams for your life. In the past 25 years of serving the Lord I have recognized when God gives me a dream He always provides a pathway to achieve it. I have also recognized that often His talents and gifts will *precede* His dreams. Very often when you are facing a *dilemma* or going through a struggle it is God's way of equipping you with the necessary tools to complete your dreams. *He is Preparing You For Promotion!* He has been laying the foundation needed to support that dream He has birthed in your life!

Matthew 25:14-30 speaks about the "parable of the talents." Jesus is speaking to the crowd and He is telling them about a man who left for a journey into a far off land; before he left he gave to his servants goods *(talents). Verse 15 says, "And unto one he gave five talents, to another two, and to another one; to every man according to his several ability; and straightway took his journey."* This parable teaches principles of *stewardship.* It examines the character of each servant and explains what they did with their talents. It distinguishes the difference between faith and fear. Two of them took their talents and multiplied them. They *increased* and *multiplied* what they had been given. However, the one servant who was given one talent went and buried it in a hole. When the lord returned and inquired of them concerning their talents and what they did with them, he was pleased with two of them. The one who had five talents gained five more, and the one who had two talents doubled them as well. But the servant who was given one talent made him very angry. Why? Because he didn't *multiply* what he had been given. The servant had a poverty mentality. He was *motivated* by fear. The result, he buried his talent. When questioned his only response was, *"...Lord, I knew thee that thou art an hard man, reaping where thou hast not sown, and gathering where thou hast not strawed: And I was* **afraid**, *and went and hid thy talent in the earth...."* His lord was infuriated because the servant did not *increase* or *multiply* his talent. He could not reward bad stewardship. He knew if he permitted this it would only encourage others to respond in this manner. Therefore only one remedy would solve this problem...*verse 28, "Take therefore the talent from him, and give it unto him which hath ten talents."*

Jesus often spoke in parables. A *parable* is a story used to teach. It has been said that a picture *paints* a thousands words. You *think* in terms of pictures. You can only move *towards* a thought...not away from a thought. Each word you speak *brushes* another *stroke* on the canvas of your mind. Jesus wanted to stress to the crowd the importance of *growth. God Requires Growth!* He wants you to bear fruit...more fruit...and much fruit. Each stage of growth requires a cutting back or a pruning process. Every stage requires you to use more of your *faith.* He became angry at the servant who operated in fear. Yes, you will make mistakes! You will even fail sometimes. But faith declares that you can always try again! You are never out with God! The only difference between failing and a failure is: *a person who fails gets back up; a failure stays down.* God expects from you a willingness for Him to develop *you* into your dreams. He will provide the *gifts* and *talents* to carry them out.

What are your dreams? To own a business? Perhaps a new job? Maybe it's a better marriage? Or is it a desire for something you've wanted from childhood? To own a home? Think about it for a moment. What are they? Now, allow your *faith* to take *action* for your dreams! Start today! Take the steps necessary to accomplish them. Write them down. Make plans on how you can see them accomplished! *First Timothy 4:14 says, "Neglect not the gift that is in thee, which was given thee by prophecy, with the laying on of the hands of the presbytery."* Paul also admonishing Timothy to stir up the gift that is in him: *"Wherefore I put thee in remembrance that thou stir up the gift of God, which is in thee by the putting on of my hands"* *(2 Timothy 1:6).* What are you waiting for? **Believe, Act, and Accomplish** all that God has birthed into your life!

STAGE # 3...THE STRUGGLE OF A DREAM

John 10:10 says, "The thief cometh not, but for to steal, and to kill, and to destroy: I am come that they might have life, and that they might have it more abundantly."

Note here: *God is the giver of our dreams, and the devil is the destroyer of them.* God gives you dreams for two reasons: so that your life might be full; and by accomplishing them you bring honor to Him. The devil doesn't like either reason. The devil also has two reasons why he tries to destroy your dreams: he hates you because God loves you; and he hates God for casting him out of heaven. He isn't strong enough to defeat God, so the way he hurts God is to cause you pain and he does this by destroying your dreams. *Consequently, your dreams don't just come to pass effortlessly; they must be fought for and taken!* God *plants* in you the dream, but you must fight for its survival and ultimate accomplishment. Your entire Christian walk from the very beginning stages requires you to battle. Paul says in *1 Timothy 6:12*, *"Fight the good fight of faith, lay hold on eternal life, whereunto thou art also called, and hast professed a good profession before many witnesses."* You are in a battle and war is being waged! If you're going to win the fight for your dreams you must know who you're fighting against. The Bible says in *Ephesians 6:12*, *"For we wrestle not against flesh and blood, but against principalities, against powers, against the rulers of the darkness of this world, against spiritual wickedness in high places."* Your battle isn't with man, but with the devil! When God plants a dream into your life, He takes you through stages of growth so you will be prepared for them. *Hosea 4:6 says, "My people are destroyed for lack of knowledge...."* I believe that many dreams are aborted in the operating rooms of *ignorance!* Many people have undergone Satan's scalpel and have allowed him to cut their dreams out of their lives. I want you to look at the life of Abraham; I believe that his life will illustrate the stages of your dreams.

I. The Stage of Obedience

Genesis 12:1-3 says, "Now the Lord had said unto Abram, Get thee out of thy country, and from thy kindred, and from thy father's house, unto a land that I will shew thee: And I will make of thee a great nation, and I will bless thee, and make thy name great; and thou shalt be a blessing: And I will bless them that bless thee, and curse him that curseth thee: and in thee shall all families of the earth be blessed."

Wow! What a promise from God! What a dream! God was ready to bless Abram; all he had to do was listen and be obedient. God places within all of us dreams that seem unachievable; this is because when we do achieve them it brings Him glory. God implanted the dream (promise); now Abram had to put it to action... he had to do something. When God gives you wonderful dreams concerning the great things that He will do for you, if you're not careful you just might find yourself sitting around with the attitude of "I'm just waiting on the Lord" when, in reality, God is waiting on you! You must put legs on your dreams! Abram wasn't satisfied with mediocrity; he was ready to step out into better things. Verse 4 says, *"And Abram departed, as the Lord had spoken unto him...."* At this time he was 75 years old. Don't allow age to hold you back! Some of the greatest achievers never achieved their dreams until they were older; one of them is Colonel Sanders of Kentucky Fried Chicken. He had failed at many other jobs, and was even fired, but he never gave up and late in years he became very successful. Abram was obedient to what the Lord had requested of him. Abram stepped out into the world of faith!

II. The Stage of Confirmation

"This is the third time I am coming to you. In the mouth of two or three witnesses shall every word be established" (2 Corinthians 13:1).

God will confirm. God will give you evidence about His promises to you. When Abram doubted his dream he would *ask* God for confirmation. God would then confirm it. To honor God for confirmation many times Abram would build an altar in *recognition* of God's faithfulness. I also believe this reminded Abram of God's goodness to him. God continually gave Abram assurance and confirmation. God called me at the age of ten; I knew then that I would be a preacher, but many times God confirmed this to me through people and circumstances. Do not close your ears to those around you; God might be trying to use them to speak to you. Whatever your dream may be... ask God to confirm it and rebirth it in your heart.

It's not wrong to ask God for confirmations. God spoke a wonderful dream to Gideon. In fact God called him a *mighty man of valor* while he hid in a stump from his enemies. *God Sees What You Can Be, Not What You Are!* Gideon asked God for confirmation and God gave it to him. I suspect that many good-hearted people have been hurt because they didn't allow God to confirm the direction of their dreams. Some may even believe that asking God for confirmations is a lack of faith. *I strongly disagree!* When you ask God to confirm something to you, you are in essence admitting to Him that you need His help and direction. God is pleased with this. God will always confirm your dreams by His *Word* first and others second. *His Word Will Always Be In Agreement!* God granted confirmations for Gideon, Abraham, Peter, Paul, Moses and many others...so allow Him to *confirm* your dreams.

III. The Stage of Faithfulness

The *trying* of your faith produces a stronger and deeper faith. However, if you didn't remain faithful during times of testing you would never know the *joy* of reward! Any successful person will tell you one of the reasons why they're successful is because they never gave up! If you're ever going to see your dreams come true, you must be faithful to each of them. *Matthew 25:23 says, "His lord said unto him, Well done, good and faithful servant; thou hast been faithful over a few things, I will make thee ruler over many things: enter thou into the joy of thy lord."* Proverbs 13:17 says, *"A wicked messenger falleth into mischief: but a faithful ambassador is health."* The main reason why dreams don't come true is because of a lack of *faithfulness* to the dream. Times will get tough. Your dreams will be challenged. You will prevail if you *remain* faithful! Faithfulness declares, *"The dream is worth dreaming!"* Times of testing and conflict are the very times the dream is taking shape and being formed. Abram remained faithful to God and continued to hold on to his promise from God. Did Abram make mistakes? Did he ever doubt? Did he ever want to quit? *Yes!* Many times Abram dealt with frustration. Abram even became impatient and tried to help God. He went to Hagar and she bore him a son called Ishmael. This was not God's *perfect* plan. Abram messed up! But he never gave up! He repented, and God forgave him and even changed his name to Abraham, which means *"father of a multitude."* Abraham remained faithful. Abraham failed God, and even lied about Sarah being his sister. He became impatient...but still he remained faithful. God knew that we would make mistakes, but He is willing to forgive them. Let God rebirth your dreams! Remain faithful to them. I waited for over ten years after God called me before my dream of being a *preacher* came to pass. Through struggles and mistakes over the years, I still remained faithful... and so did God.

IV. The Stage of God's Timing

Ecclesiastes 3:1 declares, "To every thing there is a season, and a time to every purpose under the heaven."

Have you ever felt like you just didn't have enough time? Have you ever noticed that there seems to be more things to do than there is time? Time is a precious commodity. The wisdom of Solomon recognized this very quickly, and he compared time with the seasons. What a wonderful way to illustrate how time really works. We have the tendency to categorize time as a *plus* or *minus*. *In Reality, Time Is A Stage When All Is Not Perfected, But Is Being Perfected.* Time is the gap of *waiting* for things to come to their time. Time is the *period* of waiting to get from A to Z. Time is growth!

I believe that many people give up on their dreams here at this stage. Many people get discouraged. They even get what I call ... shipwrecked faith. This is when you get tired of waiting and conclude with: God doesn't care about my dreams. You give up because you did not understand the principle of sowing and reaping. What follows sowing? Reaping? No. *Time.* Seed...*Time*...Harvest! Remember this: *time is only lost when we do nothing while waiting.*

Solomon understood that it was both very healthy and necessary to have *seasons.* He knew that every season had its *purpose.* Every season had its *time.* Allow me to illustrate this point: One of the things that I really enjoy doing is working outside in the yard. God has blessed me with a gifting in the area of landscaping. When I started working with shrubs, flowers, trees, and grass I was very uneducated about the necessary steps to insure their healthy and steady growth. I had a lot to *learn*. Because I knew that I needed help I would read and ask questions (it seemed like for one summer I hung out at the local nurseries). My knowledge increased and my landscape enjoyed the *fruits* of my labor. Believe me, it didn't happen overnight! Sometimes it was very frustrating. But as I began to *understand* the seasons and their timing, and worked with nature, not against it, things began to take shape. For instance, the best time to fertilize is the springtime; this is the time when the landscape needs more food and will grow quicker, so it is advantageous to fertilize. If you don't fertilize then your landscape won't get the best growth and may even starve. In contrast, if you fertilize too soon, then you could hurt the landscape. There is also a time to plant flowers; there are different flowers for each season. Here in South Carolina we plant pansies in the winter, geraniums in the summer; if we planted either of these out of their season they would die, because it would be out of their time. So we must work with time, not against time. God gave you time for a reason. Time allows you to learn. When you learn these lessons growth is encouraged. Is time passive? Is it waiting without motion? Is it sitting around with the attitude of "it will happen when it happens"? *Absolutely not!* Time is the gap between asking and receiving; sowing and reaping; seeking and finding. *Time Is Waiting...But Waiting In Motion! God speaks to you about His dreams for you while you're moving towards fulfilling them!*

You must see time as a necessary lapse for the growth of your dreams, and a season of maturing for the fulfilling of them. Just because God doesn't answer on our timetable doesn't mean that

He's not going to. His time is not the same as our time. God is Omniscient, Omnipotent, and Omnipresent. Let Him bring your dreams to their timing. He knows what He's doing! *Abraham* received the promise of Isaac at the age of 75 years old; he was 100 years old before it was fulfilled. *David* was about 17 years old when Samuel anointed him to be king over Israel; it was about ten years later before it was fulfilled. *Jeremiah* was called to be a prophet even while in his mother's womb; he was a teenager before it was fulfilled. *Isaiah* foretold of the Messiah to come hundreds of years before it was fulfilled. *Jesus* waited for 30 years before He began His public ministry. What do all of these have in common? They all waited in motion until the promises (dreams) came to pass. God is going to bring our dreams to pass! You must allow Him to *develop* your dreams. Allow yourself time to *grow* into those dreams. God hasn't forgotten your dreams! Allow Him to *rebirth* them! *"But let patience [a period of waiting] have her perfect work, that ye may be perfect and entire [complete], wanting nothing [fulfilled]" (James 1:4).*

When the Devil Hands You Garbage – Recycle It

"Brethren, I count not myself to have apprehended: but this one thing I do, forgetting those things which are behind, and reaching forth unto those things which are before."

Phil. 3:13

CHAPTER 2

*T*he devil likes nothing better than to have you weighed down with turmoil and confusion. His objective is to break your *focus.* When he breaks your focus, he divides your energy. Divided energy will hinder your ability to complete. He will attempt to get you thinking about *trivial* things. He never stops. He is always persistent in trying to pull you down. He will have you so wrapped up in the cares of the past that you will forget your *hope* for the future. To accomplish anything for God, you must have a clear vision and an undeterred focus on your *assignment* for Him!

When I was just a child I remember hearing our preacher, Bud Marshall, saying during the altar call, "When you bring all your needs and cares to the altar, leave them there, and don't pick up anybody else's." Does this sound familiar? God deals with areas in your life and it isn't long until new ones begin to surface. Then after you deal with much of the garbage of the past, you discover that the devil is there to hand you more. Allow me to liberate you with this profound thought: "You don't have to accept it!" There must be a time in your life when you say, *"Enough is enough!"*

I don't accept the teaching that we must always be on the defensive, constantly living in fear because there seems to be a devil lurking around every corner waiting to get you. A Church must be on the offensive taking back what the devil has stolen! We have been given a great mandate from God: *"Go ye into all the world and preach the gospel to all nations!..."* However, the only way that this can happen is for you to *put* the past behind you and press forward to the future!

The Apostle Paul was known as a great man of *faith*. Few men have known the miracle power of God as he did. But we often forget that he was human and had faults and struggles just like anyone else. Paul struggled many times with his flesh, giving testimony in Scripture declaring that the things he should do many times he doesn't, and the things he shouldn't do too often he does. Of course paraphrased. He, like all of us, had a constant struggle with his flesh. We must not forget that this man who performed many miracles also persecuted the Church with great zeal and fervency! This is the same man who held the coats of his fellow friends while they stoned Stephen to death. This man of great *faith* also possessed the intelligence to debate some of the greatest minds of that day. Often enough we choose not to see the human side of the Apostle Paul because it gives us excuses why we do so little for God. If we never see the human side of Paul we are less likely to believe that God could use us in a great way.

You might be wondering and asking yourself this question, "If Paul struggled and he had to put his flesh to death every day just like me, then how was he able to accomplish so much for God?" I have wondered the same thing myself. I have discovered that this is the very thing that makes Christianity so different from any other religion. It is profound to realize that salvation comes by faith through Jesus and His Blood. You can't earn your way to heaven. You can't buy your way either. Joining a church will not save you. You must come to Jesus just as you are and accept His forgiveness to be saved. He will use you in spite of your faults! What He is searching for is a heart that will love Him and surrender to Him. Paul was a man branded by a surrendered will. He declared by his own confession to be the bond-servant of Christ.

Paul was also so successful because he was able to forget the past. He left the garbage in the past and when the devil handed him other garbage he *recycled* it for the glory of God! When he was handed a lemon he made lemonade. Paul declares in *Philippians 3:8, "Yea doubtless, and I count all things but loss for the excellency of the knowledge of Christ Jesus my Lord: for whom I have suffered the loss of all things, and do count them but dung, that I may win Christ."* Paul's heart cry was to win Christ. He wanted to be *conformed* to His image. His focus was never broken. His goal always remained the same... *"that I may know him..." (Phil. 3:10).* We can learn from Paul through the experiences he had. Here are three lessons that Paul learned that made him more than a conqueror.

I. PAUL NEVER MADE EXCUSES.

Think about it. If you really wanted to you could think of several reasons why you can't do something. You never heard Paul say anything less than *"I can do all things through Christ which strengtheneth me!" (Phil. 4:13).* If anybody had a good reason to make excuses it would have been Paul. For example, in the book of Acts we find Paul and Silas beaten and imprisoned because they were preaching the Gospel. A demon possessed girl was delivered that day because of their preaching. They both had good reason to ask God, *"Why are You allowing me to go through this?"* I'm sure the devil was there to shout in their ears, "God has forsaken you!" Can you hear the devil screaming, "Give up! You don't have to put up with this!" I wonder how you or I would have acted if we had been beaten and thrown in jail for preaching? I can think of many times when I made excuses for much less than a beating. How about you? I don't have to name any of the variety of excuses we make to God because we're doing so little for Him. I would probably forget to remember them all. Paul and Silas didn't make any of the normal excuses that we might make. In fact, they made *no* excuses! *They did just the opposite.* They decided to have a prayer meeting. After prayer they began singing and shouting: *"And at midnight Paul and Silas prayed, and sang praises unto God: and the prisoners heard them" (Acts 16:25).* Midnight is normally the darkest time. This is the time when Satan hits you the hardest. He plants thoughts of quitting and giving up. "God has forgotten you," he says with a smile on his face. Satan will tell you that God doesn't really love you. Satan hits you hardest at this time because he knows that you're not far from a miracle. I want to make something clear here. I am sure Paul and Silas thought some negative thoughts about their circumstance. They were human like anybody else. It is not a sin to question God and wonder why circumstances might be less than desirable. Only when you let your circumstances dictate your actions is it wrong. A thought is not a sin. Acting upon any thought that doesn't glorify God is sin. The Bible says... *"If it's not of faith then it's sin...."* One of the greatest discoveries of my lifetime is... God is not moved by my needs. *He responds to my faith!* If God was moved by needs-then every hungry child would be fed. Every sick person would be healed. Every lost soul would be saved. *God Must See Your Faith To Respond To Your Needs!* Each of us have had a *midnight* experience. Most of us have failed the test. The times when things seem the darkest is when it is harder to sing praises unto God, but these are the times when it is more necessary to exalt Him! Praise gets your mind off of the circumstances. Praise changes your *focus*; your focus changes your *faith!* Praise declares to the devil what God said — I believe! Well, this book isn't about praise; however, it never hurts to remind ourselves just how powerful praise really is.

As Paul and Silas began to sing praises to God, it traveled through the anals of time and instantly they had audience with Him! *Praise gets the attention of God!* He heard. He acknowledged their faith. He responded to their cry by sending an earthquake to rattle the doors open and to loose the shackles. *They were set free!* The poor jailer — he must have thought they had escaped, because he drew his sword to commit suicide. However, the compassion of Paul caused him to cry out and say, "Stop, we are all here!" The jailer, so overwhelmed by *love,* fell on his knees and said, *"What must I do to be saved?"* Paul's response was "Believe upon the Lord Jesus Christ and you and your household shall be saved!" This desperate man reached out to Paul and Silas while they were facing a midnight hour in their life. It may be midnight in your life. Hope may be a distant memory for you. *God cares.* He will turn things around for you! *Let Him.* During the darkest hour in the lives of Paul and Silas, God chose to reveal Himself. The jailer accepted Christ and they went with him to his home where his family received Him as well. This man's home became a place for prayer meetings and Bible study. It eventually became the Philippian church where Paul writes to in the book of Philippians. What do you think would have happened if they had given up and made excuses? *You Must Realize Your Battle Is For A Reason... and It's Only For A Season!*

Maybe you're going through a midnight hour now. *Don't give up!* Hang in there! Satan knows you're in line for a promotion. God is getting ready to do something great. Don't let anything hold you back from becoming all that God wants you to be. What excuses have you tucked away into your box of *"I can't"?* How many reasons are you giving God for not trying? I've been divorced. I've been bankrupt. I was abused as a child. I don't have the money. Nobody will listen. I'm not smart. I don't have the time. I'm too fat. I'm too sick. I don't have the personality. Any of these sound familiar? If I missed any just add it to the list. The *real* truth is... the only excuse you have for failure... is *you!* The Bible says, *"That if two of you shall agree on earth as touching any thing that they shall ask, it shall be done for them...."* You and the Holy Spirit make two. Stop saying... I can't! Start believing that with God all things are possible. The devil can't stop you! *You Can Stop Yourself!*

II. PAUL LEARNED TO DEPEND ON GOD'S STRENGTH... NOT HIS.

Have you ever heard of the saying *"Let go and let God"?* How could such a simple saying be so hard? It's man's sinful nature that yearns to be in control. This problem has existed from the beginning of time. Adam and Eve had this struggle too. They were not happy with having dominion over the earth and all its creation. *They wanted more.* They wanted to *possess* the knowledge of God. They wanted control! Their lust for control blinded their sight for what was right. They were deceived by the serpent. They believed a half truth. After all, they didn't see any harm in it. We know different today. We must *learn* to sit at Jesus' feet and find contentment in Him. To really *know* victory we must know Him through obedience! This is not something that happens overnight. *We Must Learn To Lean!* Paul declares in *Philippians 3:9, "And be found in him, not having mine own righteousness, which is of the law, but that which is through the faith of Christ, the righteousness which is of God by faith."* Paul, having been taught Jewish law and doctrine, had to come to the place where he realized that the law could not save him; only dependence on Jesus could bring him salvation. We all have heard the old hymns like "Just as I am without one plea, but that Thy blood was shed for me"; "I will cherish the old rugged cross"; and none of us can forget "Learning to lean, I'm learning to lean, I'm learning to lean on Jesus...." Songs are sung with a *meaning* in mind! These songs express man's difficulty with the futile struggle with his will. *You Can Never Learn To Lean Until You Learn To Let Go!* We will never get what's in God's hand until we let go of what's in our hand. Paul understood the importance of permitting God to control his steps. When you finally arrive at a place of dependency you are declaring to God you need help. Don't always try to have things your way. His way is better. Self-will must go! Paul discovered the place where he most wanted to be — *in Him.* Stop and think about it for a moment: If you were in a relationship with the most important person on this earth. A person who had more money than you could even comprehend and possessed the intellect of a genius. Who was kind, loving, and forgiving. When His name was spoken people would stand in awe. A person who valued your friendship and wasn't ashamed of hanging around you. Most of all, He declared to the world that you were the heir to everything He had. *Wouldn't you want to be found in Him?* Paul's greatest discovery was that when you surrender to God you're really not giving up much. God *gives* much more than what we sacrifice. I remember as a little 10-year-old boy hearing preachers declare to us how much it will cost us to serve Him. They painted a picture by their words describing a God that was mean and angry. The Bible I read doesn't represent a God anything like that! When I came to Jesus I gave up nothing! My self-will had to go. It would have gotten me in trouble anyway. I said "yes" to God! *He wants what's best for me.* He's not mean or angry! I agree with Paul. I want to be found in Him. I am depending on His strength to carry me through the toughest of times. To be found in Him where there is peace and fulfillment. I'm not ashamed of the Gospel because it is a light unto my path and a lamp unto my feet. The Gospel has the power of God to bring *life* to the lost! *Victory* to the victims! Deliverance to the captives and sight to the blind! Go ahead and get up and shout, "Praise the Lord!" Paul knew the importance of being found in Him. Most of all Paul knew the joy of giving up all he was and gaining everything that Christ is!

III. PAUL LEARNED TO LIVE BY FAITH.

Smith Wigglesworth had a famous saying he would often declare to his audiences while preaching. He would say, *"You can shout as loud as you want; God won't hear. Show Him your faith and you will get His attention with all of heaven!"* Paul understood that kind of faith.

Hebrews 11:1 says, "Now faith is the substance of things hoped for, the evidence of things not seen." It continues to say in verse 6, *"But without faith it is impossible to please him: for he that cometh to God must believe that he is, and that he is a rewarder of them that diligently seek him."*

Hebrews chapter 11 is known as the faith chapter; if you want to be *edified* take time to read the whole chapter. Like anyone else Paul had to learn to *walk* by faith. So do we. Many people today believe they have to see it... to believe it. You will never *recycle* the garbage of the past with that attitude. To walk in fullness of life you must learn to walk by faith.

Let's look at what faith is not. Faith is not fate. If you sit around and do nothing then nothing will be done. *A Seed Of Nothing Creates A Harvest Of Nothing!* You can't have the mentality of "I'm just waiting on the Lord." *This is not faith.* Faith is not fiction. You're not entering into a world of fairytales when you *exercise* your faith. Faith is not something only to consider in your far off dreams. Faith is *now!* Faith is not presumption. If you walk out in front of a car intentionally don't expect to survive because you believe that you're walking by faith. If you write a bad check for $7000.00 and don't have the money in the bank, please don't declare you're walking by faith. You are walking in presumption.

I think that you have a good idea what faith is not. Let's define what faith is. *Faith Is The Distance Between God And Man!* Faith is fact. Fact that is based on the Word of God. Here are four steps to *unlocking* the flow of faith in your life.

Step # 1 Faith Is The *Substance* Of Things.

Substance *means* essential part. God always gives you something to work with...an essential part. He gave Moses... a staff. David... a slingshot. The Widow Woman...a vessel of oil. The Shunammite Woman...a room for the prophet. The Young Lad... two fishes and five loaves. You have something in your hand right now that is *essential* to unlocking your faith. What is it? Look around you. Take inventory today. God promised that He would give you seed...a seed is something you *sow* to create a harvest. It is essential to your faith. *Do Not Inventory What You Don't Have... Look At What You Do Have!*

Step # 2 Faith Is Something *Hoped* For.

Faith is *hope*. What things are you hoping for? A new job. A better marriage. Salvation of a family member. More money to buy the things you want. Hope is reaching. Hope is believing that your circumstances will be better. Hope believes in dreaming! *Hope Is Rejecting Your Senses And Embracing Faith!*

Step # 3 Faith Is The *Evidence* Of Things Not Yet Seen.

Faith is evidence not yet *revealed*. When you first started believing God for something, the evidence was not tangible yet. Faith is believing that what you're asking for will *become* tangible. For example, let's assume you went out to buy a car today; however the color you wanted wasn't available. The dealer told you that he could order the color you wanted and have it in two months. You give the okay, and the car gets ordered. You don't have the car now, so does this mean that you're not getting the car? *No.* It only means that it has not arrived yet. You're confident that you're going to get it. The dealer said that he had ordered it, and it was on its way. So you took him at his word. But you can't see the tangible car. You can't ride in it. You can't even touch it. However, you tell all your friends that you have it. Have you lied to them? Are you deceiving them? *No.* Why? Because you believed what the dealer told you and you agreed to wait. Based on this man's word, you agreed to wait. *You took him at his word!* What does the Bible promise you? What does it say about your desires? Search diligently. Document every promise. Journal every request made. God cannot lie! *Take Him At His Word!* **Take Note:** I want to be very clear here. I'm not saying that you can order anything you want and God must deliver it. Your desires must *parallel* the Word of God. Faith is based upon what He said in the Bible...*first!* Look to Godly counsel...second. Inventory and count the cost...third. Finally, do you have a peace about it? *Peace Is Chief!* Faith is not something you use as a tool to get what you want anytime you want it. God will only honor your faith as you walk in His *will* and when you're obedient to His Word. Faith is what God *equips* His Church with to accomplish His will. *With Faith Nothing Is Impossible For The Believer!*

Step # 4 Faith Is... *Now.*

"Even so faith, if it hath not works, is dead, being alone. Yea, a man may say, Thou hast faith, and I have works: shew me thy faith without thy works, and I will shew thee my faith by my works" (James 2:17-18).

Faith is *today.* It isn't yesterday. It will not be tomorrow. It is today. This moment. Right now! Faith takes action! *You Must Move From Where You Are Today To Get To Where You Want To Be Tomorrow!* Faith doesn't sit around and say, "I'm just waiting on the Lord." Faith waits in motion. God will unfold His plans as you walk according to what you know now. It is like the game of checkers. You move... then God moves. Faith is a continual process of learning. Faith *waits* on God for more information, while *acting* upon His last instruction. You must be doing something. If you are asking for a better job, then begin by looking for one. If you want more knowledge, then go to school. If you want to lose weight, then join a gym. If you want to make friends, then be friendly. You must do what you know to do and then God will make up the difference. Begin today. Don't procrastinate. Take action! Talking about it won't bring it to pass. Tomorrow is too late. *Faith Is Now!*

One of my dearest friends is Dorothy Spaulding — I believe she's a modern day Corrie Ten Boom. She's a remarkable woman of faith! Seven years ago she and her husband, Russell stepped into Augusta, GA and declared, "God told us to start a Christian TV station." People laughed at them and said that they would never survive! One local television celebrity even announced live on the air one night, *"TV-36 will be off the air soon...they'll never make it!"* Yet, Russell & Dorothy forged ahead with very little resources within their reach, and without the big budget most network television stations have. The finances were not within their reach, however, faith was in their heart — which was enough. Through their determination and unwillingness to follow the voices of the crowds, they obeyed God and stood firm in their faith. Today, in Augusta, GA WBPI-TV49 is a station that broadcast to thousands of viewers each night, and reaches into homes touching lives through television. She recently released her book entitled, *"We Walk By Faith..."* This book chroncles her and Russell's journey of faith that brought them to where they are today. It's a must read to anyone who wants to see faith walked out. Write: Dorothy Spaulding P.O. Box 3618, Augusta, GA. 30914-3618

The Apostle Paul knew and understood all of these steps. He recognized that each step was just as important as the other one to his faith. He was careful to include them all. This is why he was able to turn his garbage into glory! He knew that with God nothing could stop him. It didn't matter what the devil threw at him. Paul knew that God could turn every experience into something good. *God Can Turn The Memories Of The Past Into Your Hope For The Future!* ~**Todd Coontz**

Pain – The Forgotten Teacher

"My brethren, count it all joy when ye fall into divers temptations; Knowing this, that the trying of your faith worketh patience. But let patience have her perfect work, that ye may be perfect and entire, wanting nothing."

James 1:2-4

CHAPTER 3

*W*hen you think of the word *"success"* what comes to your mind? Is it pictures of extravagant homes? Maybe exotic cars? What about large bank accounts? Probably so. You will probably think about the same things most people associate with the word success. We never think about the homeless person or a single mother. Our minds never consider the uneducated to be a success in life. Instead, we consider the accomplished, talented and well polished to be successful. Only those who have reached the height of their profession are worthy of such a word. We think of the grandeur of fancy restaurants and of luxury. A place where smiles and happiness co-exist. We never once remotely consider the word *pain.* Hollywood has played its part in this misconception of success. The daytime soaps are very popular. People watch them because they find it easy to escape the hustle and bustle of the real world. They find themselves drifting off into a world of make believe. A place where you never confront your problems; you only forget they exist. It would be great for a world like this to exist. But it doesn't. Is what I just described success? This is what most people believe when they think of the word success. The American dream. An accumulation mentality. I must admit that I'm not any different than anyone else. I like nice things. I shun the remote possibility of experiencing pain. When it comes my way I'm not too thrilled about it. I don't wish it upon anybody. But the fact is we will never be totally free from pain while we live on this earth.

Let me share some humor with you that will help illustrate my point. I remember when I got this crazy idea to begin lifting weights (I think all men have gone through this at some time). I had decided that I would look bulky with protruding biceps. I could even envision myself getting clothes tailor made because of my bulking masculinity. The picture I had painted in my mind was much easier than real life action. Each day I would make my way to the gym ready to carry out my mind's picture of a well-tuned body. Each day when I went to the gym, before entering the place where all the weights were, I would pass by this sign that read, *"NO PAIN, NO GAIN."* Oh, I hated that sign! But with its simplicity was a profound statement. Without pain there can really be no true growth. Struggle is part of life. Incidentally, while lifting weights I hurt my back. Even though the sign wasn't talking about physical injury, the pain in my back serves as a reminder that it does hurt to grow. I know now what Paul was talking about concerning a thorn in his flesh.

When rewards are handed out at banquets they are given to the best and most accomplished of our day. You will hear about the great things that so-and-so did. We will stand and clap for their great achievements, never hearing about the pain they faced along the way to accomplishment. The rigors of battle and the difficulty they faced are never mentioned. We only hear about their success. I believe we often do this because in our minds we must think if we don't acknowledge pain then it will go away. But it never does and it's not long before we're facing a difficulty again. My purpose in writing this chapter is to help you to recognize that pain can be a teacher. While none of us want to face it, we must acknowledge that it's unavoidable. If we can't avoid pain, then why not learn from it. Pain is not foreign to any of us; it passes all language barriers and is not prejudiced because of race, sex, or religion. Please allow me to share some reasons why God allows us to suffer pain. I believe that it will both edify and encourage you. Remember, pain is not to be ignored, but is to be taken as a tool to make you better and richer for each experience.

I. PAIN TEACHES US THANKFULNESS.

"Giving thanks always for all things unto God and the Father in the name of our Lord Jesus Christ."
Ephesians 5:20

"Whatsoever ye do in word or deed, do all in the name of the Lord Jesus, giving thanks to God the Father by him" (Colossians 3:17).

We can never really know the *joy* of true happiness without having a thankful heart. *Pain teaches us thankfulness.* It doesn't matter the source, pain helps us to look beyond our abilities to the abilities of someone greater. Think about it. If you never experienced sadness how would you know if you were happy? If you never felt the struggle of battle then how would you know the taste of sweet victory? If you never felt the pain of rejection then how could you know love? If you never experienced loss then how could you understand gain? It's true opposites attract. However, never forget that opposites also bring balance. The real lesson that pain teaches us is to take a step back and consider the needs of others. It *reminds* us to be thankful for what we have today. Pain teaches us to have a thankful heart.

II. PAIN REMINDS US THAT
WE ARE ONLY HUMAN.

Mankind possesses what we know as an ego. Sound familiar? Call it pride... self-confidence... determination... good attitude... or nothing-is-too-difficult-for-me mentality. It all means the same — self ego. When God's blessings come our way we sometimes get the idea that somehow we made it happen. No one else — just me. If we aren't careful we sometimes will lose sight of the giver and only see the gift.

I want to share with you at this time just how this book came about. All through this book I will be sharing my personal experiences with you. Some of them have been very difficult for me to endure. But through each circumstance I have become a more sensitive person to the needs of others. Tremendous growth has taken place in my life. My prayer for you is that God will use me to help you *grow* and become more like Him. I want to share with you some of my personal testimony.

God saved me at the tender age of ten. I remember walking down the aisle of a backwoods country church heated only by an old potbelly stove. I guess the reason why I remember the old stove is because during our winter revivals if you sat too close to the stove you would get burnt — needless to say, I've been burnt. God's hand moved mightily during those nights of revival; the presence of God was so thick at times, I believe that you might have been able to cut it with a knife — I wish I had tried now. I was saved on a Friday night. I can still remember walking down the aisle hearing that old wood beneath my feet squeak after each step I took. God touched me that night and little did I know that I would no longer be the same. I went home that night with a new handle on life.

The following night a transformation took place that was almost as good as the night before. You see, my parents were told by doctors that I was hyperactive — really I think my mom already knew this because I was much too active. As a child I struggled with a number of things. It was very hard for me to concentrate for any extended periods of time. It was extremely brutal for me to sit still for more than ten minutes. The result of these struggles made it difficult for me to learn. In elementary school I was placed in several "special" classes to try to help me keep up with my peers. I still remember even after twenty-seven years the names of my teachers. I had trouble with Reading, Math, English, and especially Writing...this one's funny since this is my second book I'm writing. I flunked the second grade...twice! I was always getting in fights at school...and losing. *I was struggling!* I had gone through a variety of tests by Navy doctors who diagnosed me to be hyperactive. The end result was they prescribed for me a drug called Ritalin; this was supposed to help me concentrate better and make me more calm, and I believe it did. Allow me to pause for a moment and offer this encouragement to the parents who may have children who may be hyperactive. I know at times your circumstance may seem unbearable and there seems to be no hope in sight...but God will help you. I also believe that God can heal your child! You must realize that God has given you a *special* child who has abilities and talents that far outweigh their disabilities, and who someday, if managed with lots of love and patience, can become anything they choose to be. Look at your situation as a *tool* for developing a future leader who someday will have the ability and energy to make a difference in society. Looking back now at the days of my childhood I realize that God has used my situation to my benefit; it has made me a better person. Being hyperactive didn't take anything from me, but added to my character as a person. I gained much more than I felt I had lost.

Each day at my middle school a teacher would walk me to the office, where my medication was kept. I remember walking to the water fountain with my fists *tightly* closed holding my medicine. Many times I felt as though I could feel every student's eyes glaring at me as though I was a freak or at the least a sideshow in the circus. It was very humiliating. Children can sometimes be very cruel with the words they say, and whoever made up the saying "Sticks and stones may break my bones, but names can never hurt me" — well, that person was never called names before. *Names do hurt!* Because of my condition my peers wouldn't include me in their games very often, and when they did, I was almost always picked last. The result...I became a loner. It became easier and easier to hide my true feelings and just go around with the attitude of just not caring. You see, to really love or care you must first be willing to be hurt — I had been hurt one too many times. As I began my walk with the Lord, God began to put back in me a *love* and *compassion* for those who seem unlovable. God used these circumstances to build within me steel determination which has helped me to become a leader. These leadership qualities have allowed me to make tough and sometimes unpopular decisions. *My Pain Has Become A Bridge Into My Future, And A Barricade From My Past!*

The second night I found myself walking down that same squeaky floor to an altar to ask the God who saved me if He would also heal me. In fact, I was so sure that He would that I brought my bottle of pills with me and handed them to the preacher and said, *"If God can save me, then He will heal me too!"* The preacher said, "Todd, He certainly will." Reverend Bud Marshall laid his hands on me and asked God to deliver me...and He did! That night I walked away from that worn-out altar leaving my bottle of pills behind me and my future before me. *Glory to God!* I have never taken a pill since.

The pain I felt taught me perhaps one of the greatest lessons a child of God must learn. That is, before you can be anything great for God you must acknowledge that you're only human. Why is this so important? Because if you cease to acknowledge that you're only human then your need for God will diminish. God cannot use somebody who thinks that they have everything in control. You must declare, *"More of You, Lord, all I want is more of You!"* By realizing that you're only human you allow yourself room for mistakes. This helps you to never get the attitude of being self-sufficient, therefore allowing God to work through you as well as in you. Pain *reminds* you that you are indeed human. You have made mistakes in the past, and you will even make mistakes in the future. Remind yourself when faced with failure that God isn't looking for robots, but humans that He might show His love and willingness to forgive. So forgive yourself! *God has.* He still has a plan for your life.

"And we know that all things work together for good to them that love God, to them who are the called according to his purpose" (Romans 8:28).

"Being confident of this very thing, that he which hath begun a good work in you will perform it until the day of Jesus Christ" (Philippians 1:6).

III. PAIN BUILDS CHARACTER.

"A good name is rather to be chosen than great riches, and loving favour rather than silver and gold."
Proverbs 22:1

"But let your communication be, Yea, yea; Nay, nay: for whatsoever is more than these cometh of evil."
Matthew 5:37

The Bible speaks very *candidly* concerning the issue of being honest and forthright in conducting your affairs in life. The Bible doesn't open this subject up for debate. As Christians we must have a code of ethics that sets us apart from all others. The world must recognize that there is a difference in us; if they don't it will be harder to reach them for Jesus. We have the greatest gift to offer a dying world, but they won't listen if they don't see a change in us. Charisma is not enough! *We must have character.*

We will examine this more closely, but let's first see how the dictionary defines the word character — *a trait or distinctive combination of traits.* You are known by your traits and how you conduct yourself in life. People identify you by your traits... good or bad. The way you act says something about you. Do you get mad easily? Are you always late? How often are you rude to people? Do you respond in love? Do you tell the truth, or do you sometimes tell little white lies? What is your temperament like? How do you respond under pressure? All of these questions will provide answers for people about you. What you are like determines your effectiveness in reaching people. *Your Good Intentions Do Not Decide Your Actions...Your Character Does!* From the beginning of your Christian walk God endeavors to *mold* you and make you into His image...or His character. This is known as the growing stage. We grow from babes in Christ to full mature Christians. *It is a progressive process.*

God spoke to a young man that He called to the prophet ministry even while in his mother's womb — Jeremiah. Just like anyone, he had to *grow* and learn. God spoke to Jeremiah one day and prodded him to go to the potter's house to watch the potter at work. Jeremiah was obedient and he went to the potter's house to see what God wanted him to see.

> *"And the vessel that he made of clay was marred in the hand of the potter: so he made it again another vessel, as seemed good to the potter to make it. Then the word of the Lord came to me, saying, O house of Israel, cannot I do with you as this potter? saith the Lord. Behold, as the clay is in the potter's hand, so are ye in mine hand, O house of Israel"* (Jeremiah 18:4-6).

The very first thing that Jeremiah saw was a *marred vessel.* God wanted to illustrate to Jeremiah the imperfections of man when we first come to Him. We are all marred in some form or fashion. Before we can get help, we must first acknowledge that we need help. God, like the potter, will mold us and shape us into an *excellent* vessel. He is looking for teachable students. There can be no excuses for not coming to God and allowing Him to use us. God was also teaching Jeremiah to recognize who was doing the shaping...the potter. The hands of God do the molding and shaping of our character. He often uses circumstances that are painful to bring about this growth. While the potter works on the clay, if it becomes marred he will take the clay and slap it back onto the wheel for reshaping. I'm sure there have been times in your past when you've felt like you have just been slapped on a wheel... it hurts. *If God Cushioned Every Blow, Then You Would Never Learn To Grow!* The potter is very patient and he will continually shape and reshape until he is pleased with his work. The Bible says that God is both patient and long suffering. We must always remember that man often gets weary and tired, but God never does. God will never give up on you! Allow God to mold and make your character into His image so that you can be found wanting nothing. God's will is to make you a whole and complete person.

The Apostle Peter is a great example of someone who had character flaws, but was also willing to allow God to work in his life. Peter's first encounter with Jesus was while he and his brother Andrew were fishing.

"And Jesus, walking by the sea of Galilee, saw two brethren, Simon called Peter, and Andrew his brother, casting a net into the sea: for they were fishers. And he saith unto them, Follow me, and I will make you fishers of men" (Matthew 4:18-19).

The Bible says in verse 20, *"And they straightway left their nets, and followed him."* Jesus' only requirement of them was to follow Him. We often forget that God is the one who does the work in our life; we can't make it happen without His help. God is not searching for completed vessels, only willing vessels.

Peter has been characterized as someone who was very hot tempered. He was a fighter. He had the attitude of let's act first, then ask questions later. He was impatient. When Jesus was in the garden of Gethsemane and the Roman soldiers came to take Jesus away, Peter was very quick to take out his sword and slice off one of the servant's ears. Really, Peter wasn't trying to just cut off an ear; he was trying to kill him. We know this because of the way the Roman sword had to be held. It was custom for the Romans while in battle to take the sword with both hands and drive it down the middle of their enemy. Jesus picked up the servant's ear and put it back on. Jesus then said to Peter, "If you live by the sword, then you will die by the sword."

Even though Peter was rough around the edges, the one characteristic that he did possess was he had a heart for God. God had spent much time with Peter teaching him and showing him the way, patiently building character in his life. The big mistake that we all remember about Peter was when he denied Jesus three times. Even before it happened Jesus had told Peter that he would do this, but just like Peter he denied it strongly. When it did happen we find Peter brokenhearted and crushed. I'm sure that this was the lowest time in his life. I know that he experienced a pain that he would never forget. I'm sure that there were thoughts that he could never be anything useful for Jesus, and the devil was there to torment him and declare to him that he was a failure! Just because you fail it doesn't make you a failure. Failure will only last as long as you permit it! Even though Peter thought his days of ministry were over, little did he know that they had just begun. God was working behind the scenes to mold and make his character into a useful attribute for His glory. Even though Peter had failed God and found himself denying His Lord, God was still in control and He had placed in position yet another plan. A plan for Peter's success! Peter would do great things for the Kingdom! God didn't write Peter off His list for greatness and neither are you written off!

There is not a better way to conclude this chapter than by looking at Peter the finished vessel. We find in the book of Acts that the day of Pentecost was fully come and that the Holy Spirit came in full power. The Bible says in Acts 2:3, *"And there appeared unto them cloven tongues like as of fire, and it sat upon each of them."* It was such a move of God that devout Jews made fun of them saying they were drunk with new wine. Now we find a different Peter than the one who had denied Jesus three times. Acts 2:14-16: *"But Peter, standing up with the eleven, lifted up his voice, and said unto them, Ye men of Judea, and all ye that dwell at Jerusalem, be this known unto you, and hearken to my words: For these are not drunken, as ye suppose, seeing it is but the third hour of the day. But this is that which was spoken by the prophet Joel; And it shall come to pass in the last days, saith God, I will pour out of my Spirit upon all flesh: and your sons and your daughters shall prophesy, and your young men shall see visions, and your old men shall dream dreams."* Peter preached that day with boldness and a fire that he didn't have when he denied Jesus. But God completed a work in his life, shaped his character, and transformed failure to victory! That day the Bible said that 3,000 were added to the Church. Peter realized that yesterday's failure can become the catalyst for tomorrow's success! I want to encourage you not to give up, because even though you may have failed in the past, the pain you feel will not last forever. Remember that your pain is often a bridge, not a barricade, to success! Very often the circumstances that you think will be your demise will turn out to be the instruments for your success! Learn from your pain and allow it to teach you the greatest lessons that you will ever learn!

Three Foundations of Life

"And, thou, Lord, in the beginning hast laid the foundation of the earth; and the heavens are the works of thine hands: They shall perish; but thou remainest; and they all shall wax old as doth a garment; And as a vesture shalt thou fold them up, and they shall be changed: but thou art the same, and thy years shall not fail."

Hebrews 1:10-12

CHAPTER 4

*M*y father-in-law is a builder by profession. He builds custom homes in Aiken, SC, and has been in business since 1965. He has worked hard over the years to establish a good reputation and is known as one of the best. It wasn't until I met him that I realized just how important the foundation really was, and how much detail went into getting it done right. I want to share this information with you so you can understand the significance of a good foundation.

The very first thing that has to be done is the land must be surveyed; this tells you where you can put the house and where your property line starts and ends. There are always County and City restrictions that you must abide by. These restrictions are there to assure you'll find the best place for a foundation at the location. When you have determined where you are going to place the foundation... the work begins. Bulldozers and dump trucks come rolling in and the work starts. After the land has been cleared, it is important to walk over the area where the structure will be built and examine everything. You then will lay out markers for each corner. So that you have proper dimensions you create a structure around the foundation using two-by-fours. This will help guarantee that the length, depth, and height are exact to your plan specifications.

Once your structure has been completed you will then dig the foundation out, making sure that the footers are exact in their depth and width. This is important so you'll pass final inspection. Finally, when you are sure that you've met the building codes, you'll call for the cement trucks and you pour the concrete into the foundation. In a couple of days, after the concrete has set up, you'll call for a final inspection. If you passed, a building permit is issued and you can start building your home.

As you can see, it doesn't happen overnight. There is preparation and a great deal of time involved to assure that you are successful in building your structure. The foundation is critical to the survival of the structure. It will only endure the test of time if it's done right! This foundational principle is equally important to your journey through life. You must have a good foundation if you ever hope to do something significant with your life. Your foundation is vital to your growing process; a faulty foundation will affect everything in your life. *Your Foundation Determines Your Future... And It Will Decide How You Respond To Your Past Failures!* **~Todd Coontz**

With the foundation being so critical to your success, it makes good sense to allow the Master Builder to lay it in place. As I experience growth in my life I have become more aware of how crucial it is to allow God to *lay* the foundation. The same remains true about understanding that only God is qualified to lay a proper foundation. We must set aside our self-will! Our abilities to make things happen can sometimes hinder God from working His foundation in us. *Become Pliable So You Can Become Usable!* There are three foundations that are laid during our lifetime. They are essential to our growth and development as a Christian. God uses each of them to transition us from point A to point Z. They are stages of growth and are necessary in our learning process. However, the message I want to communicate to you is no matter how faulty your foundation is, God is still laying another foundation to assure your success. The foundation that God lays is the best! God wants to transition you from where you are today. He will use the foundation from your past to lay a foundation for your future!

I. THE FOUNDATION THAT SOMEBODY ELSE LAID

You really didn't have a choice whether to be born or not. Somebody else made that choice for you...your parents. After birth... life began and a foundation was being laid. This foundation originated as an embryo and was nurtured by somebody else. Our parents were our first influence in the beginning. They helped shape our character and our habits. As we spent time with them we learned and were taught their belief system. Our foundation was laid based on their education, experiences, prejudices, attitudes, and religious beliefs. Still, there are others who have contributed to our initial foundation, such as friends and relatives. Our schoolteachers and coaches. Our pastor or youth pastor. Athletes and our heros. Our mentors. Sadly, the biggest foundational influence is found in almost every room in a house...TV. Modern television has become our closest friend today. Through television the liberal media has had the opportunity to promote their agendas and infiltrate the minds of modern society. Their beliefs, which in many cases are anti-God, are conveyed to be absolute truth. Pictures are painted in our minds from what we see and hear. They are shaping our thinking process based on what they believe and were taught.They accomplish this while we're in the privacy of our homes. Foundations are laid. Futures are formed!

Hopefully by now you're beginning to understand how important a good foundation really is. We have learned that a foundation is something that you build upon. It's strength and whether it was laid correctly are very crucial for long term success to be guaranteed. Your temperament, beliefs, ethics, attitudes, and experiences all make up the ingredients in your foundation. They determine the strength of your character...*your character determines your success!* How you will act and react to people, places, and things is also determined by your character. They make up what we know to be your personality. They are laid from the beginning by all that I have previously mentioned. Every person who has influence in your life and each experience that you've gone through will shape your personality and character.

I see a lot of my father and mother in me. My father has always been a hard worker. As a child I can remember seeing him always doing something. Now that I'm an adult I find it very difficult to sit around doing nothing...this is because of my father's influence. He was also a very kindhearted and faithful person; these are characteristics that come naturally to me now that I'm an adult. I was influenced by him because of two reasons. First, I was around him all the time and I learned from simple association. Second, I loved and respected him. Because of these two reasons a foundation was laid in my life. My mother always saw the good in everyone she had ever met. I remember in grade school we would sometimes get substitute teachers and there was a particular one nobody liked. However, it was always easy for me to be kind to her because of what I had observed in my mother. I don't have time to share all the wonderful traits that my parents have passed down to me — it would take too long — but I do want to share one more. My mother has a degree in interior decorating, and I remember as a child that she was always doing something new in our home. She loved to decorate and found it to be a gifting from the Lord; she could decorate like nobody else. Without giving it much thought, after we built our new home, I discovered that I enjoyed decorating our home, and have been told that I was very good at it. You see, my mother had laid a foundation in my life and I didn't even know it. We learn from those we are around. Foundations are laid by the circumstances and people we surround ourselves with.

We can all tell stories about the difficulties we faced as a child. We can all remember times of great pain and circumstances that literally changed our lives — good and bad. We can look at our characteristics and see our strengths and our weaknesses because of someone with whom we had close contact. Because of the bad influences of others there are places in our foundations that need to be fixed and strengthened. Although you had no control over who would be laying your foundation from the beginning... *you do now!* God can take each circumstance and bad experience and turn it around. You can go forward with God by simply allowing Him to bring healing to your life; however, you must walk in forgiveness. You must realize that it is God who has ordained your life. It is God who has breathed life into you. God doesn't want to replace your foundation... but build upon the good that is already there. God wants to build upon the foundation that somebody else laid!

II. THE FOUNDATION THAT
WE ENDEAVOR TO LAY

Have you ever had expectations that didn't come true? We have all planned our careers based on our dreams. From grade school all the way through high school we've chosen classes that would complement our plans for our chosen careers. Do you ever remember somebody walking up to you and asking you what you wanted to do with your life? And you gladly responded usually with something lofty at first: "I'm going to be a doctor, or maybe an astronaut." *You* had your life all planned out. You knew exactly what you wanted out of life. You had your hopes and dreams... your future was just ahead of you.

The hardest struggle we have as a believer is the struggle with our will. All of us have all these things that we want and want to do, and it is very difficult for us to lay this aside and say, "Lord, Your will." We have our way and God has His! So the struggle starts and we begin a fight between the flesh and God. We now endeavor to become the builder and we set out to construct and lay the foundation. After all, we know more than God!

It is sad because much of our Christian walk is found to be doing what we want, going where we choose to go, and living how we see fit. We will go to church faithfully, we will pay our tithes religiously, and we will endeavor to be kind to our neighbor. What more could God possibly ask of us?! Much of our preaching never touches the area of denying self and taking up the cross to follow Jesus. We would rather hear preaching on subjects such as "Keys to Financial Prosperity," "Keys to Defeating the Devil," "How to Get Healed" and many more good and necessary topics, but somehow the messages of self-denial and a price to pay are avoided and never addressed. I believe in and preach about financial blessing, walking in healing, kicking the devil, victory over sin, and get excited about them! They are Biblical and necessary. The tragedy is that few know God in depth and can really feel His heartbeat for intimacy. You can never know God because of His wonderful works; you must know Him because of His ways! His ways teach us about Him. His works tell us of His goodness and mighty power. To know God we must allow Him to lay the foundation. But still this is a struggle for us.

I believe the reason that we have so much struggle with allowing God to lead us, aside from our self-will and sin nature, is that we don't have a clear picture of God's mighty power! We rebel against Him because we have never really understood God's attitude towards us. We think for some reason that God doesn't want us to be happy. In our minds we think that God couldn't possibly give us things we want. We have been taught that God will only meet our needs, not our wants. Sound familiar? So from the very beginning of our ability to lay the foundation we automatically do what we want versus what God wants because we think that He has it in for us. If we ask God He will only tell us about things that will rob us of joy and fun. Our mentality is that God is out to get us. So the struggle continues!

There is nothing we can do about the foundation that someone else laid; we can only take what's good and build upon it. However, we can do something about the foundation that we endeavor to lay. We can build it God's way! But first we must see God as He really is. When we have a clear picture of the Master Builder then it will be easier to trust Him. Psalm 25:8 says, *"Good and upright is the Lord: therefore will he teach sinners in the way."* God is good! Psalm 23:1-6 declares, *"The Lord is my shepherd; I shall not want. He maketh me to lie down in green pastures: he leadeth me beside the still waters. He restoreth my soul: he leadeth me in the paths of righteousness for his name's sake. Yea, though I walk through the valley of the shadow of death, I will fear no evil: for thou art with me; thy rod and thy staff they comfort me. Thou preparest a table before me in the presence of mine enemies: thou anointest my head with oil; my cup runneth over. Surely goodness and mercy shall follow me all the days of my life: and I will dwell in the house of the Lord for ever."* This sums it all up! God wants what's best for you! God wants you to be happy! God's will is better! God's foundation is a foundation of joy, peace, and fulfillment! So what are you waiting for? Get self out of the way, and let God have His way!

III. THE FOUNDATION THAT GOD LAYS

"Teach me thy way, O Lord, and lead me in a plain path, because of mine enemies" (Psalms 27:11).

"Nevertheless the foundation of God standeth sure, having this seal, The Lord knoweth them that are His...."
2 Timothy 2:19

We have previously discussed two foundations: "the foundation that someone else laid" and "the foundation that we endeavor to lay." The final foundation is the most important to the survival of our life. The third foundation doesn't take away from the good of the first two, but adds to them: The foundation that God lays. There is so much that I want to share concerning this topic; my prayer is that God will guide me to share only as He wills. I can share much on this subject but need only to share what's relevant. God saved me and healed me when I was 10 years old, as I have already shared in a previous chapter, but also God called me to preach as well. The third night of the revival where I was both saved and healed, I found to be the place where I preached my first message. Imagine a 10-year- old preacher. I was scared and during the whole message I wound my Timex watch. The message wasn't new but the messenger preaching was. I preached on Moses and the Ten Commandments; I was very familiar with this subject because I had just seen it on TV. You see, even then God was laying a foundation for the time of my first message. If I hadn't seen the television program I might not have had anything to say. I remember it as though it was just yesterday: the message wasn't long, but it seemed to be an eternity. Strangely enough, the people sat there in awe because I'm sure that they hadn't seen anything quite like that. I still remember my closing statements. I said, "Moses came from off the top of the mountain and found them worshiping a golden calf; he became angry and threw the Ten Commandments down on them and blew them all up!" Well, it wasn't totally Biblical (thank God) but the people heard a different perspective anyway. After I had said all of that I remember looking over the audience and saying, "That's all I have to say." I wasn't as well read in the Bible as other preachers were, but at least I knew when to shut up and sit down — ha! ha! Behind the scenes God was laying a foundation for a young preacher to be. A foundation that would stand sure!

As I grew older there were more opportunities for me to preach. I remember hanging around every preacher I met so that I might learn more about God and His Word. I grew physically and spiritually and at the age of 16 years old I began preaching quite often. Preaching was my life; it had become my life's goal and ambition! I knew without any doubt that this is what God wanted me to do. So everything that I would do was geared towards reaching and fulfilling that call. All through high school I could hardly wait until the time when I could say that I was a full-time preacher. I was anxious, excited, and very impatient! I even had a habit of getting ahead of God. I bet none of you have had this problem. Well, I made it through high school and found myself attending Bible college. Even then I was only there because God had told me to go.

After finishing Bible college I finally found myself in fulltime evangelistic ministry. I had waited 10 years for the fulfillment of this call. It was finally here! I started out at the age of 20 years old traveling as God opened the doors, preaching the Good News! I preached wherever God gave opportunity, in all kinds of denominations, on the streets, in tents, in store buildings, on a one-to-one basis. If you stood still long enough I would be preaching to you! God told me to go preach and I took Him at His Word!

After traveling for about three years I found myself getting invitations to appear on a number of Christian television programs; this was something God brought about. I enjoyed it and it gave me opportunity to minister to larger audiences. In 1988 I was asked to be a guest on Channel 38 in Pittsburgh, PA. Russ Bixler was the founder of the Christian station. That night I preached and then was interviewed by Stan Scott. I so enjoyed getting the opportunity to meet Stan (he was kind of a celebrity). God gave me favor with him and his wife and he was very instrumental in getting me an invitation to go to Ohio. I was invited to go to Canton, Ohio, and be a guest on a Christian program called "The Plus or Minus 60 Show" with Denny and Marge Hazen. God moved mightily during the program so I was asked to stay a few more days to preach. I did and it worked out that I became a regular guest there preaching and sharing the Gospel! Behind all the scenes even from my childhood God was laying a foundation for my success! God blessed each program and I came to really enjoy the television media for propagating the Gospel. I remember after having been there for about three months I had an invitation to go to Pennsylvania to preach. While driving on my way to the meeting I remember having such a contentment and even saying to God, "Lord, I wouldn't

TODD COONTZ

want to be doing anything else." Boy, at the time I didn't really know what God was up to!

God was behind the scenes laying a foundation that would take me to another level of maturity and growth. I had received an invitation to travel to a small southeastern town in South Carolina, Aiken. I started the revival with great excitement because I felt like television was giving me opportunities that I wouldn't have had — I was in Aiken because this preacher's son had told him about me; he had seen me on television. God moved during those nights of revival. I soon discovered that the preacher was going to resign as pastor and he wanted to know if I was interested in taking the church. I replied very firmly and quickly, "No, sir!" There were two things that I said that I would never do: I would never live in the South, and I would never pastor a church! I bet you can guess what I'm going to say next. God began to deal with my heart concerning Aiken and He gave me such a burden that when I drove around the city I would weep like a baby! As hard as I tried, I couldn't shake the burden! Years ago I learned a valuable principle about God, He won't ask you to do anything until first He gives you a burden. God won't make you do anything; He will give you such a burden that you will want to do what He is asking of you. God was putting the foundation in place. I told God that I would do what He wanted and about two weeks later I was voted unanimously in as pastor of that small southern church.

Little did I know that my life as I knew it would be turned upside down! I came to Aiken with fervor and zeal and loads of confidence. I had come with the objective that with God's help

- 66 -

we were going to take this city for God! "Devil, get out of my way; Todd's in town now!" I preached my heart out! People got saved and the church began to grow! People had asked me about how large of a church that I was believing God for; I said, "5,000 at least!" I have never had trouble believing God for impossible things. I have seen God do some very impossible things from my childhood and up. So a measly 5,000 wasn't anything! My life was about to change. God's foundational plans were different than mine.

I'm not going to go into lengthy detail about all that happened, but what I will say is everything went wrong that normally goes wrong in church. As time passed troubles began to surface. I tried to deal with them the best I knew how but being only 23 years old I discovered that people had a hard time respecting my decisions. Besides, I had made several wrong ones that caused some people to lose confidence in my ability to pastor. God was turning my life inside out! Without going into any detail because I don't think that it will do any edifying to do so, I will say that I made my share of mistakes. I wasn't to blame for everything because much happened as a result of the devil trying to control the church, and in order for him to do that he uses people. Strangely enough, when God moved the strongest in the services is when the devil fought the hardest. Problem after problem arose and because of my young age and lack of experience they only got worse.

After nine months of fighting and never gaining ground, many people were hurt and the scars in my own life ran very deep. I resigned as pastor. I felt like a total failure, my confidence was gone, my hope was lost, and in my heart I felt as though I had really let God down. I was a basket case! I was very near to a nervous breakdown. But still God was laying a foundation. God still had an open door for me!

Through my struggles I have learned that even when we surrender our lives to God and declare to Him, "Your will, not mine" that doesn't mean life will become easy. God never once made a promise to us, "If you give your life to me then there will be no more pain, disappointments, and troubles." He never promises to keep us from hurting. He never implies that the road you take for Him won't be rocky. It might even seem like a dead end! When God lays a foundation He uses lots of different tools to construct it, some of which hurt. What God wants are vessels that will be willing to grow in every circumstance, who won't give up, no matter even if it's your fault. God will still use you if you will let Him. God lays the foundation, so He already knew what would happen. He has made provision for your success and growth!

I had left Aiken a brokenhearted, wounded, and an "I have failed God" preacher. Went home where I found lots of love and understanding from my parents. I was only gone for about two months when God began dealing with me about going back to Aiken. There was a fear in me that I was fighting; the devil was telling me all kinds of things — none were good. In my mind I thought that I would never see Aiken again, at least I hoped I wouldn't. But God wouldn't let it go and after being gone for three months, I found myself back again in Aiken, SC. I'm not going to go into detail of how it all came about because I don't feel that it's necessary. What is important is the end result of this story. I did come back to Aiken and it has been five years now since I pastored that small church. I really haven't been involved in full-time ministry for the past five years. There were a lot of hurts and wounds that God wanted to heal. Let me say this to all the preachers that are reading this book. The fact that you're not pastoring now, or you're not involved in "full-time ministry" — what I mean by this is you're not making your livelihood solely from ministry — doesn't mean that you've failed God or that you're not as important as someone whose livelihood is dependent on the ministry. Don't let people or the devil tell you those lies! I believe that at times it is not only healthy but necessary to set yourself aside for a time to get healed and to grow. God's will for your life and His timing will not be the same as for someone else's. So sit still and let God touch those areas in your life that are not pleasing to Him, and allow Him to prune your branches. The foundation that God has been laying for me over the past five years has to do with growing in Him. Before everything happened, because of preaching for so long I had found my identity in preaching, not in Him. If I wasn't preaching then I wasn't happy. God sat me still and wanted me to learn that the ministry couldn't flow through me until it had been done in me. Your ministry should be a by-product of what you are, not what you do. I had to learn to be content in just knowing Him! I am. God also wanted to teach me other things. There were some character flaws that God wanted to get rid of. One was pride. I really never knew that it was in me until all this stuff happened. It was. God took it out. I also believe that there was a growing-up that I had to do. I was very mature spiritually, but there were practical things I needed to learn. It hasn't been easy, and at times it has hurt, but the past five years of my life have been the best yet. Even though I haven't been preaching, my walk with God is much richer and fuller! I'm becoming more completed.

IV. THE COMPLETED FOUNDATION.

"But the Lord is faithful, who shall stablish you, and keep you from evil" (2 Thessalonians 3:3).

Without a Foundation, Even Castles Are Little More Than Piles of Stones — Stability and Structure Come Before Elegance and Beauty. The first four chapters of this book was written in 1995. Although they've been edited slightly, I've endeavored to keep them as original as possible. The reason I've chosen not to rewrite them entirely was because during this time in my life God was still healing, shaping, and molding me into His character. I wanted you, the reader, to *experience* through these written pages the emotions and growing process that I was feeling. These first chapters represent an incredible transition time in my life. A time of change and with it always comes uncertainity — not really understanding what God's really doing. And yes, even discouragement, pain, struggle and victory. This was a time when I truely had to depend on His wisdom and will. What does the Bible call this? Oh...I remember now — FAITH!

From this point on every chapter was written in the year 2002 — seven years later from my first manuscript. You will still read about the things I've learned, fortunately hindsight will reveal another perspective with more detail and objectivity. My prayer remains the same for you — learn from my experiences and know that God's working in you. Growing is a process of becoming — *to be* means you've arrived. Don't give-up on this process! I think that you will recognize the growth in my life and you'll see how God used every experience in life — good and bad — to mold and shape you into His image. Although I have a lot to learn, I've learned much already. God is continuing the process of preparation and His pruning sheers are still razer sharp. God hasn't changed and His requirements for a productive life remains unchanged to — fruit...more fruit...and much fruit. Growth is the fruit representing a life of hurt, pain, struggle, and victory! When you allow God to deal with the closed closets of your life — He can *Open* the Doors into Your Victorious Future!

A final note before closing out this chapter. God's call and gifts are without repentance — meaning that He will never take them back. Look at my life, God called me to preach at the age of ten, and still today that call rests on my life; however, I haven't been preaching for over twelve years. *Why?* Because God's message never changes — His methods do. I believe the day that God called me to preach He placed within me every gift, talent, ability and anointing to accomplish every assignment that He would ever ask me to complete. He knew then what I'm now discovering today. Life is a journey which represents a collection of your personal experiences as you see them through your eyes of learning. God is revealed first to you, and secondly in you. As you walk out His will according to each experience He brings in your life He shapes you into His character. Today, God has me traveling and teaching (preaching) His message of prosperity to His people. My twelve silent years represented a time when God was perfecting His call and will for me today.

The Joy Of Completion

*"But none of these things move me, neither count I my life dear unto myself, so that I might **finish** my course with **joy,** and the ministry, which I have received of the Lord Jesus, to testify the gospel of the grace of God."*

Acts 20:24

CHAPTER 5

*W*hat things have you left undone lately? How many projects have you started that are still unfinished? How many books have you purchased that remain on the shelf gathering dust? All of us can offer excuses: *"I will get to it later or tomorrow."* Still, closets remain cluttered. Promises are broken. Commitments go unfulfilled. Tasks are left incomplete. Dreams are never accomplished. *The list goes on...and on...and on.* I'm sure you'll agree with me that it's much easier to start than it is to finish. No matter how good your intentions may be...nothing can replace the *fortitude* to finish. I've included this chapter in my book because this area in my life was frustrating and a great challenge to me — mostly because my understanding of how to successfully start and finish each task was limited. Really, I failed to recognize the distractions that would come while attempting to finish or accomplish something of significance. I can even remember my high school principal telling me, *"Todd, you seem to lack fortitude."* This statement then caused me to think that in order to have it you must be born with it. It is in your genes, and I simply wasn't one of the fortunate ones who possessed this great quality. Consequently, I just gave up on believing that I could ever become a finisher. This attitude sabotaged some of my success in early life. What does fortitude mean anyway? Webster's Dictionary defines it as: *strength of mind or character.* Most of us have strength of mind; however, this is commonly known as stubbornness. Incidentally, stubbornness is not a synonym for the word *fortitude.* Stubbornness means to be unreasonable. The correct meaning of fortitude is....*follow through.* The determination to *complete.* The attitude... *"I'm not resting until the task is finished!"*

As I got older I discovered that fortitude was not the missing link in my life. In fact, while I was attending Bible College, two of my friends, Bob and Eric, had written something in my yearbook that confirmed this: *"Todd, we know that you will succeed in life because you have steel determination."* They recognized something about me that I failed to see about myself. I finally realized that everyone is capable of becoming a finisher. However, it is your responsibility to develop and equip yourself with the keys necessary to finish. Everyone can become a person who starts and successfully completes each task or dream they have. You too can experience the *joy* that comes through the act of finishing!

Someone once said, "Success is ten percent *Inspiration,* and ninety percent *Perspiration,"* I believe it! When we take a closer look at the life of Paul it becomes very evident that he's driven with a passion to complete. Look at what he writes to the Philippian church.

> *"Brethren, I **count** not myself to have apprehended: but this one thing I do, **forgetting** those things which are behind, and **reaching** forth unto those things which are before"* (Philippians 3:13).

Here we find the Apostle Paul very active. He is *counting...forgetting...*and *reaching.* All three are action verbs. He is not just sitting around. *He is acting!* Why? Because Paul was a finisher! I believe there are three keys available to you as a Christian that will unlock the doors that have been closed in your life. Paul discovered and used these golden keys to great accomplishment. He reaped the *joy* which follows every act of completion. Let's look at each of them so you too can *experience* the joy that comes after completion. They are: 1) *The Key of Precision*; 2) *The Key of Resolution*; 3) *The Key of Reaching.*

I. THE KEY OF PRECISION
...COUNTING THE COST

> *"Brethren, I **count** not myself to have apprehended..." (*Philippians 3:13).

Precision is a noun that means...*exactness.* Paul clearly understood the importance of accuracy. He knew the necessity of counting the cost. He recognized that every endeavor would cost something. *Nothing is ever free.* Accomplishment always requires time, energy, money, and even great sacrifice. Paul knew and accepted this as part of the price required to be paid in exchange for the joy of completion. He also knew that he hadn't apprehended it either. But he was definitely *pursuing!* Paul examined his life and took inventory of what was in his future. He knew that he didn't want to continue down the road he had traveled most of his life. Damascus was not his future. He wanted more. He wanted peace. *He wanted joy!* So, he counted the cost. What would it take for him to finish? How much would it cost him to serve Jesus? I'm sure that Paul's mind was asking him many questions; however, his heart only delivered one answer... *"I press toward the mark for the prize of the high calling...."* All questions asked and answered.

Jesus made it very clear to all that would follow after Him that it would cost them something. In fact, *everything.*

*"For which of you, intending to build a tower, sitteth not down first, and **counteth** the cost, whether he have sufficient to **finish** it?"* (Luke 14:28).

Evaluate...calculate...and determine how many steps you will be required to take to achieve the act of completion. *The Key of Precision Demands Your Accuracy!*

One of the great accomplishments of my life was becoming a private pilot. I value it so much because it represents some of the most difficult times of both *learning* and *discipline* in my life. I was very fortunate to have an excellent instructor (Don Barnes); he was very patient with me and explained everything with detail and accuracy. I'm a slow learner; however, I'm also determined and committed to learning. Accuracy and precision are a must when it comes to flying an airplane. Words like *almost* and *just about* simply do not cut it. For example, imagine yourself boarding an airplane to take a trip for a badly needed vacation. While en route to your destination the pilot clicks the intercom mike and says, "I have bad news...it seems as though we are going to run out of gas before we reach our destination; however, I just wanted everyone to know that we *almost* had enough gas to finish our trip." How would you feel about that statement? Or perhaps he was wrong and you made it all the way to the airport; however, you fell short of the runway fifty feet. Would you feel any better because you *just about* made it to the runway? Good pilots are precise, accurate, ritualistic, ceremonial in habit. They leave nothing to the fate of chance.

Before I fly any trip, there is planning involved. I calculate how much fuel the trip will require. I will check the weather forecast both from my departure and destination, because airplanes do not like thunderstorms. *I don't either.* I will calculate the weight and balance of the plane to be sure that I do not overload it. I will make certain the plane has had its 100 hour inspection along with the required annual inspection. Then I will walk to the airplane and walk around it examining it closely for any potential problems. Finally, before takeoff, I will also go through what is called a checklist, which includes several other steps too numerous to name. This may seem like it takes hours to complete, but this really only takes about 30 minutes. But this could easily be the most important 30 minutes of the trip, because I might discover something that could prevent me from making a successful trip. Learn the *discipline* of precision. Accomplishments are the result of good habits. The purpose of a habit is to create discipline. *What habits have you created on your journey to completion?*

II. THE KEY OF RESOLUTION
...TO DECIDE WITH CERTAINTY

"...forgetting those things which are behind..."

Philippians 3:13

Forgetting the mistakes of the past is one of the hardest things to do. Yet all of us have things in our past we are trying to forget. *I know I do.* Some are haunted by the memory of a tragedy that has created enormous pain. Many are forced to live with the consequences of their youthful mistakes. Still others have buried their pain so deep they don't even realize that many of their reactions in life are due to unforgivable mistakes from the past. Of course, everyone deals with the temptation of sin. Struggle, temptation, and pain are a natural process of life. Everyone faces them; however, not everyone faces them the same way.

Throughout the annals of time mankind has encountered every kind of disappointment imaginable. Sadly, many are left with scars which remain very sensitive and hurt that reaches the deepest corridors of the heart. Paul, just like us, had to deal with things from his past. Some things were brought on by himself, while others were just a part of the process of life. *Still*...they were memories he wanted to forget. Before his dramatic Damascus *experience* he was a persecutor of Christians and many were put to death because of him. On one occasion he even held the coats of his peers while he watched them stone Stephen to death. Yet, you find him writing to the Philippian church telling them that he made a decision to simply forget his past mistakes, *"...forgetting those things which are behind...."*

The ability to *forget* could perhaps be the most important key on our journey to completion. *Why?* Because you must first learn to forget your mistakes in order to move beyond your past. However, you can't forget until you first learn to forgive yourself. Paul learned this and accepted the forgiveness of God. This truth: learning to accept God's forgiveness is the real message of the work that Jesus *completed* at Calvary. Paul understood this valuable truth and this revelation alone brought him to the place where he could say,

> *"And be found in him, not having mine own righteousness, which is of the law, but that which is through the faith of Christ, the righteousness which is of God by faith"* (Philippians 3:9).

Paul had tried to *work* his way into righteousness; however, this proved to be futile. Paul finally discovered what the law failed to recognize...*salvation is through grace*... not works. This revelation changed his perspective and his goals.

> *"That I may **know** him, and the **power** of his resurrection, and the **fellowship** of his sufferings, being made **conformable** unto his death"* (Philippians 3:10)

Paul *surrendered* to Jesus' will and he received what the law couldn't provide...*forgiveness.* Paul's heartbeat changed. He wanted to *know* Him! To know His *power...fellowship...*and to be *conformed* to His image. Paul found relationship with Jesus. Religion did not bring him fellowship or joy. *Jesus did!* I have discovered three things that we must do to move beyond our mistakes and into a place of forgiveness. I have personally applied these truths to my life and they have brought me for-giveness and joy. Each truth will bring to *you* a fresh revelation so you too can *experience* the joy that comes through forgive-ness.

1. Man Will Always Mess Something Up.

This cardinal truth dates back to the very beginning with Adam and Eve. Read the Bible from cover to cover and you'll discover this truth for yourself. The Bible catalogs man's failures as well as his victories. Multitudes of books have been written over the years; however, none of them chronicles the faults or shortcomings of man like the Bible does. This alone makes the Bible unique. One of the greatest discoveries of my lifetime is this very truth: *man will always mess something up.* It took me some years to realize this. In reality, I think that some things can only be learned with time and age...this perhaps is one. Why is it so hard for man to acknowledge this truth? *Man messes up.* To grasp this truth you need to understand its origin. Pride and self-will. There is not a better illustration of this than the example found in Matthew, chapter 19.

> *"And, behold, one came and said unto him, Good Master, what **good thing** shall I do, that I may have eternal life?"* (Matthew 19: 16).

If you've been in church for any length of time you've heard the story about the rich young ruler. However, I think that most have failed to really recognize what his real problem was. Most think it was his money. By the way, get my book, *7 Myths About Money;* it will give more detail about the subject of money. I

THE JOY OF COMPLETION

don't believe his problem was money. Money was merely a symptom of a more severe problem...*pride*. Pride has always been the root of man's unwillingness to admit his mistakes. The rich young ruler asked Jesus, *"What good thing shall I do...?"* This man wasn't seeking the forgiveness of Jesus. In fact, he didn't believe that he was doing anything wrong. His *posture* proves this by his first statement, *"...Good Master...."* At first glance this seems like a very innocent statement; however, it exposes his real heart. Calling Jesus good wasn't the problem; it was when he elevated himself to be equal with Jesus. How? By his first question, *"What good thing shall I do...?"* This rich young ruler called Jesus "good" then immediately proceeded to ask, *"What good thing can I do?"* Look at this closer...Jesus is a *Good* Master...and this ruler wanted to do one more *good* thing...the two parallel one another. The ruler compared himself with Jesus as... *good.* He was looking for *another* good thing to do to earn salvation, therefore suggesting that salvation could be earned. He wasn't seeking salvation...*he wanted equality!* Jesus observed how this young man approached Him, and He recognized his real attitude by the first question he asked. This is *why* Jesus answered him with such a direct and harsh statement:

> *"...Why callest thou me **good**? there is none good but one, that is, God..."* (verse 17).

Jesus *knew* that He was God. But, to prove a point and to reveal this ruler's heart Jesus responded appropriately. And, to further prove this, you find Jesus instructing him to obey the commandments...He named six of them. The rich young ruler answered Jesus saying, *"All these things have I kept from my youth up....*" He must have first thought, "Wow, it can't really be this easy!" Then he asked Jesus, *"What lack I yet?"* Here is where it gets interesting. Jesus simply looked deep into this man's heart and offered him the solution.

> *"Jesus said unto him, If thou wilt be* **perfect***, go and sell that thou hast, and give to the poor, and thou shalt have treasure in heaven: and come and follow me."*
> Matthew 19:21

Jesus diagnosed the problem, and He offered the remedy; however, this young man was unwilling to walk away from his money. His heart was revealed by his actions.

> *"But when the young man heard that saying, he went away* **sorrowful***: for he had great possessions"* (verse 22).

Jesus never wanted his money. He only wanted his heart. Although, Jesus offered this young ruler the opportunity to be perfect *(complete),* his pride and self-will wouldn't allow him to let go of his god...*money.* He may have been obeying the six commandments that Jesus mentioned; however, he was breaking at least one of the commandments: Thou shalt have no other gods before me." *Pride* keeps many from moving beyond their past and into their future. You must first admit that you can't save yourself, and you need forgiveness; then you can receive what Jesus is offering you.

Paul possessed *resolve.* He knew that he needed help. Only when he decided to walk away from his pride and self-will could

Jesus really help him. Look at what he tells the Philippian church.

> *"But what things were gain to me, those I counted loss for Christ."* (Philippians 3:7).

> *"...I count all things but loss...I have suffered the loss of all things, and do count them but dung, that I may win Christ"* (verse 8).

We need to say like Paul, *"I count all things but loss!"* What things are holding you back from God? Is there anything that you're unwilling to walk away from? *What is it?* When you *surrender* to His will, and obey His instructions, you will receive what only He can offer you...*forgiveness.* Please, don't allow pride to keep you from all that God has for you. Decide with certainty that you will walk in forgiveness, make up your mind to forget your past, and walk away from pride and self-will. Then you can say with Paul, *"...**forgetting** those things which are **behind,** and pressing **forward** to those things which are **ahead.**" Man Always Messes Up; Jesus Never Fails!*

2. You Have An Advocate When You Sin.

> *"My little children, these things write I unto you, that ye sin not. And if any man sin, we have an **advocate** with the Father, Jesus Christ the righteous."*
>
> 1 John 2:1

Take note: This particular verse was written to the *Christian*...not the unbeliever. Look at it closer. He addresses this letter to...*my little children.* Who? *The believer.* Jesus died for your past, present, and future sins.

What is an advocate? Mr. Webster says: *one who pleads the cause of another; to defend.* When we sin John says we have an advocate...*Jesus.* What a wonderful promise of God! Jesus is your defender. He pleads your case before God. It is the devil who accuses you. When we sin we are promised forgiveness.

*"If we **confess** our sins, he is faithful and just to forgive us our sins, and to cleanse us from all unrighteousness"* (1 John 1:9).

Confess your sins. Ask Him to forgive you. Accept His forgiveness. And you will be on your way to living a *victorious life!* You will begin to experience the joy of completion.

3. God Doesn't Remember Your Sins...Why Should You?

*"...saith the Lord: for I will forgive their iniquity, and I will **remember** their sin **no** more."*

Jeremiah 31:34

God has a bad memory! When you confess your sins, God promises to remember them no more. The key here is you must *confess* your sin. What mistakes have you made in your past? What sin torments you? Simply confess them to God. He will forgive and forget. *When the Devil Reminds You of Your Past, Remind Him of His Future!*

Consider this. Judas betrayed Jesus and Peter denied Him three times. Both of them made horrible mistakes. Judas betrayed Jesus and sold Him out for thirty pieces of silver, and Peter denied Him openly and validated it by cursing. Both mistakes by Judas and Peter were despicable! Yet their mistakes each yielded a completely different result. Judas' mistake yielded unforgiveness and death, while Peter's yielded forgiveness and increase. Why such a difference in results? Simply because Peter chose to forgive himself and forget his mistake. *Judas could not.* Don't allow your past mistakes to hold you back from what God has for you. He doesn't remember them, so why should you? Forgive yourself and choose to forget every mistake that is holding you back. *You Can't Reach For The Future While Clinging To The Past!* ~**Todd Coontz**

III. THE KEY OF REACHING
...TAKING ACTION

"...reaching forth unto those things which are before."
Philippians 3:13

Reaching is proof that you haven't obtained. Newton's law of physics says...*for every action there is a reaction.* But there can't be a reaction until there is *ACTION!* Have you ever heard the expression "talk is cheap." *It is.* There is a time to discuss, evaluate, gather information, and plan. However, there is also a time to implement your plans based on your research and information. A time to take action! Nothing can ever replace this vital step. You can never experience the joy of completion without first taking action towards finishing.

Recently, I was invited to teach on the subject of money in Greenville, SC, at WGGS TV-16. Dr. Jimmy Thompson started that station over thirty-plus years ago and it's one of the oldest continuous Christian stations in America today. He has pioneered seven high power stations like WATC TV-57 in the Metro-Atlanta, GA, area along with several low power stations. He has personally helped numerous religious broadcasters to get their start in Christian TV. Dr. Thompson also pioneered and pastored Faith Temple Church for over thirty-plus years, and in 1957 he started Faith Printing, Inc. The night I was invited to appear with him I arrived about an hour early. I remember walking towards the bathroom through a big room (it wasn't a hallway) where the walls were covered with pictures. All four corners were filled from top to bottom. The pictures represented over thirty-plus years of Christian broadcasting ministry. The pictures that layered across the walls looked like a who's who of Christianity. Names too numerous to mention...people you would know...people who have made a tremendous impact on society. And in almost every picture was Dr. Thompson with a smile on his face.

Dr. Jimmy Thompson has dedicated his life to ministry for over fifty years. What an incredible life this man has lived! I remember standing there and staring at the cascade of pictures that covered the walls and thinking...*here's a finisher.* As I stood there in awe of the life this man has lived the Holy Spirit gently tugged on my heart and asked me this question: *"What is the difference between the man who strikes out at home plate and the runner who gets thrown out at third?"* I responded, "The only difference is the runner on third got a little exercise." Then the Holy Spirit simply said to me, *"Todd, it's not how you get started that matters, only how well you finish!"* I asked God to help me to become a finisher.

Later that night Dr. Thompson invited me to his office where we talked till almost midnight. We discussed a variety of topics; however, I was very interested in discovering his keys to great accomplishment. I believe that when you're given an opportunity to spend time with great achievers you should learn from them. And you almost always learn by asking questions, then allowing them to answer and do most of the talking. So I did.

It was obvious to me that Dr. Thompson was a man of action. What personal keys did he use to unlock the doors of success to become a finisher? *I wanted to know.* What I discovered was amazing! Through the course of our conversation I discovered like so many others I've studied Dr. Thompson practiced the same habits. *Truth always remains constant!* In reality, what became more apparent to me was that there were three enemies to action or finishing that everyone faces. Let's look at them together. The three enemies to action are: 1) *The Enemy of Procrastination;* 2) *The Enemy of Perfection;* 3) *The Enemy of Overload.*

THE THREE ENEMIES TO ACTION

1. The Enemy of Procrastination...the act of delaying.

*"And that, knowing the time, that now it is high time to **awake** out of sleep..."* (Romans 13:11).

Perhaps the biggest enemy to action is *delay.* There is a time to discuss your next move. A time to calculate and plan. And there is a time to gather needed information. But after you have discussed your options, calculated, planned, and gathered information there is only one thing left to do...*take action!* Talking about it won't get the job done. Asking more questions will not complete the task. Telling everyone what you're planning to do simply won't bring about results. Reminiscing about what you've done in the past won't change the present. There is only one solution...*take action!* What have you been putting off for another day? Make your list. Document the things that need to be completed. Then get up and move towards completing each of them one by one! Take baby steps one foot after another. How do you eat an elephant? *One bite at a time.* How do you build a house? *One brick at a time.* Start...Begin...Get going. Take action! Paul did.

2. The Enemy of Perfection...to be flawless.

"...that ye may stand **perfect** *and* **complete** *in all the will of God"* (Colossians 4:12).

Hard to believe? Perfection an enemy. *Yes.* I believe many people fail to take action because they believe their result won't be good enough. They think that no matter what they do it won't quite measure up. Many simply don't start because of the fear of imperfection.

To understand what the writer of Colossians was saying we have to first define the word perfection. Webster defines perfection: *flawless; unblemished.* Know anyone like this? Of course not! Perfection is an impossibility. It can't be attained. Would God ask you to become something that you're incapable of becoming? Absolutely not! Then what does it mean to be perfect? I'm glad you asked. There are two plausible meanings. First, the word perfect means to become complete, the emphasis put on the word *become*. Second, it also can mean *excellence*. Let's look at both of them in more detail.

First of all, God doesn't expect perfection from you. He does expect you to continuously be in a state of becoming. What does it mean to become? To become means to reach for more than what you are presently. Everyone wants to *be*; hardly anybody wants to *become*. The best way that I can explain this is through an illustration. Georgia isn't far from my house and this state is known for her beautiful sweet peaches. One beautiful spring day my wife and I decided to visit a peach orchard in Georgia. After arriving there we were walking and holding hands when we noticed that the trees had begun to bud. I grabbed one of the branches to take a closer look and then turned to her and said, *"Honey, I think that this is the most **perfect bud** that I've ever seen."* A couple of weeks later we decided to return to the peach orchard to take another romantic walk, but now the trees had blossomed and were covered with beautiful white blooms. I looked at my wife and said, *"Wow, I think that these are the most **perfect blooms** I've ever seen!"* Later in the summer my wife and I got up early one Saturday morning and headed out for the peach orchard once again, but this time we were going to sample a peach. Upon arrival my wife and I raced over to the orchard and I removed a beautiful, plump, sweet Georgia peach from one of the trees. While holding it in my hand and looking at it closer I said to her, *"This is the most **perfect peach** that*

I've ever seen." How could this peach be perfect on three different occasions? Because during each stage of growth it became what God intended it to be. First a bud, then a bloom, and finally a peach. It started small and became what God intended it to be in time. *It matured.* For every season of life there is a stage of growth and there is a different expectation placed upon us according to each level of growth. Wouldn't you expect more from a teenager than you would a child? Your walk with God is progressive and at different stages of growth. You will never attain perfection, but you can *become* complete. Every task, each assignment, whatever you need to accomplish, God only expects you to do your very best. Perfection is not part of the equation...so don't let it hold you back!

The second plausible meaning would be *excellence.* What does it mean to be excellent? Does it mean to be perfect? Without a flaw? Without any mistakes? *No.* Excellence means: Superior...Top-Notch...Cut above...Grade A. Just to name a few synonyms. It is the opposite of mediocre.

To be an excellent person means to always be in a state of *becoming* better. You are always looking for ways to improve yourself and everything you do. It requires you to offer your very best with what you have today. None of us have an unlimited supply of money. However, you are always giving your all with what resources you have presently. Are you an excellent person? Have you been giving your all lately? Start today. You can experience the joy of completion!

I want you to get a tape series from Pastor Robb Thompson. I have had the opportunity on several occasions to spend time with him. He is the most "excellent" person I know today. He is an expert on the teaching concerning excellence. Write him today for the tape series entitled *"Becoming a Person Of Excellence*. Family Harvest Church 18500 92 Avenue, Tinley Park, IL. 60477 Phone (708) 614-6000, $30.00.

Decide today that you won't allow perfection to become an enemy to action. You can become *complete,* and with every task, assignment, goal, and dream you can accomplish them with *Excellence!*

3. The Enemy of Overload...too many things.

Have you ever felt like there just wasn't enough time in a day? There are only two possible reasons why you would feel this way. First, you have not learned how to manage your time efficiently. Second, you have scheduled too much...you have *overloaded* your time. There is only so much sand in the hourglass. *You must decide who and what gets it.* Many never take action because they are trying to accomplish too much at one time. Here are four keys to help you avoid overload: 1) *Set Priorities;* 2) *Eliminate Unnecessary Stuff;* 3) *Learn To Say No; 4) Incorporate Others To Help You.*

FOUR KEYS TO AVOIDING OVERLOAD

KEY # 1... SET YOUR PRIORITIES

Set priorities based upon God's list and what brings you the most reward. If you don't...someone else will. Everyone is abiding by some kind of schedule. It can be productive and fruitful, or it can be sloppy and incomplete. *You decide.* For example, if you team up with someone who doesn't respect time, then your time will be disrespected also. You let them know that this is how much time you're willing to spend on any particular project; if you don't, then your time will be lost forever. You must take control. List your priorities from most important to least important and do them first. A husband will have responsibilities to his wife, and a wife to her husband, children to their parents, employees to their employer, and employers to their customers, etc. Everybody must set their priorities in order. There are always more things that you can be doing. You must decide what is important and what will bring you the most reward. *Prioritize or someone else will!*

KEY # 2...ELIMINATE UNNECESSARY STUFF

Eliminate unnecessary stuff. A well-rounded diet requires proper portions of the right kinds of foods. Elimination is as important as nutrition. The body simply eliminates what it can't use or doesn't need. *You should do the same.* Awards are never given for how much stuff you're doing, only for what you have completed. If you overload yourself with too much, then nothing will get your full attention. Only commit to something that you can give your all to. Rarely does anything receive all of you...if you overload yourself then it will fall to zero. *You must decide!*

KEY # 3...LEARN TO SAY *No*

Learn to say No. It's not a bad word, you know. You can always be doing more than you're doing now. The question is...are you doing what's important? Nancy Reagan had the right idea in the eighties in her war against drugs...*Just Say No.* It really works well. And it frees up your time and schedule tremendously. *Try it.*

Right now...today...you can apply all of these keys and experience the *joy* through the simple act of completing. You too can become a finisher! I like what Paul wrote to Timothy: *"I have fought a good fight...I have finished the race...and I have kept the faith...now waiting for me is a crown of righteousness."*

KEY # 4...INCORPORATE OTHERS TO HELP YOU

There are two kinds of people: 1) Those who decrease your time 2) Those who increase your time---you must discern which kind you want around you. Highly productive people are master's at delegating. The recognize the value of someone who is qualified to help. This is an important key to accomplishment. Why? Because everybody has a need to contribute back to society. Man's very nature has a desire to produce...increase...and multiply. *Think about it?* When are you most content with yourself? When you feel like you're making a difference. Right? God has gifted everyone with talents and abilities so that you can become a highly productive person within your field of expertise. My wife, Dana is a perfect example. She enables me to complete so much in a day because she helps me in more ways than I can document. She never complains, and always is looking for ways to help me. She increases my time through her help and her love. Stop...Look...and listen for clues! There are people that God has sent into your life to help you complete your task with excellence. You must discern who they are!

Experience: The Tardy Teacher

"Wisdom is the principal thing; therefore get wisdom: and with all thy getting get understanding."

Proverbs 4:7

CHAPTER 6

*W*isdom is when we learn from someone else's mistakes.

Knowledge is when we learn from our mistakes.
Experience is a name everyone gives to their mistakes.

Everyone is learning. The real question is, *"How are you learning?"*

📖 *Wisdom is learning by the mistakes of others.*
📖 Knowledge makes you a participant.

📖 *Wisdom helps you avoid loss.*
📖 Knowledge educates you through loss.

📖 *Wisdom brings promotion.*
📖 Knowledge brings experience.

📖 *Wisdom uncovers answers by asking questions.*
📖 Knowledge discovers answers through each experience.

📖 *Wisdom brings understanding.*
📖 Knowledge is the search for understanding.

📖 *Wisdom is the road less traveled.*
📖 Knowledge is the road most traveled.

📖 *Wisdom is the principal thing.*
📖 Knowledge is the next best thing.

Truthfully, all of us learn through both wisdom and knowledge. All of us like to think of ourselves as being wise. Yet the evidence of our mistakes dictates otherwise. Other...wise meaning *knowledge.*

YESTERDAY'S NEWS IS OLD NEWS

New information is key to our learning process. Without it life becomes nothing more than a collection of our past memories. We must have information on a daily basis. Why? Because some information changes daily — time...day...news... etc. Yesterday's news is old news. Events...schedules...deadlines are all based on information. Information is important to your success. It's the difference between poverty and prosperity, and between failure and success. Your "today" chronicles yesterday's decisions based on retrievable information.

Because...*what is retrievable is usable.* However, missing information is as bad as unusable information, or old. Your "tomorrow" will be a collection of what you've learned today. Your learning process is based on information that is being supplied to you. Wrong information can be costly, devastating, and even life threatening. Correct information can create wealth, detour a possible catastrophe, and give life. What information have you been getting lately?

We are living in a time when information is so readily available to us. The information highway makes accessible to anyone who possesses nominal computer skills any kind of information possible with just a click of the mouse. For those less daring individuals who don't possess these skills, the media of television, newspapers, magazines, and radio offer yet another flavor of information for your intuitive minds.

BILLIONS ARE SPENT ON LEARNING INFORMATION

I recently read that the United States spends more money on learning information, which we call *"education,"* than all other countries combined. Billions are spent every year for the propagation of information. Spies are trained and sent out in hopes of seizing "top secret" information. Laws are passed to guard against unfair financial advantages in the stock market, such as the "Insider Trading Act," which protects certain nonpublic information. One single piece of information can make all the difference. For example, the other day I was eating at my favorite Chinese restaurant. The owner came to me to express how much she appreciated my business. Because I'm a financial advisor people sometimes ask me for free informa-tion. This was one of those times. After talking to her briefly, I discovered that she was missing information about certain tax laws concerning her investments. It ended up costing her thou-sands of dollars in taxes. *Why?* Because she structured her in-vestments wrong, and it cost her dearly. Missing information is costly! *Something You Don't Know Is Robbing You Of Some-thing You Want!* ~**Todd Coontz**

LEARNING IS A LIFETIME PROCESS

Whether you consider yourself to be a scholar, student, pupil, or disciple, the information you embrace deter-mines your future. So it's important to make sure you're learn-ing the right information. Learning is the key that unlocks the doors of opportunity for you. Learning is a lifetime process. It's not a destination; it's a journey! Now, learning is a twofold endeavor: First, you learn as a protege, which is *an obedient learner.* Second, you also learn as a mentor, which is *a trusted teacher.* Everyone should become both a protege and mentor simultaneously. You should posture yourself as a student as well as a teacher. I have had several mentors in my life. All of them have taught me many valuable lessons. Again, learning is a lifetime process...*I'm still learning today.* I want to help you to achieve the highest level of learning...*Wisdom.* My prayer is that God will use these five keys to unlock every door that's been closed. *Wisdom is the Principal Thing!* Knowledge is the *next* best thing.

FIVE KEYS TO LEARNING

KEY # 1...You Must Have A Teachable Spirit.

"For whom the Lord loveth he correcteth; even as a father the son in whom he delighteth" (Proverbs 3:12).

*A*re *you teachable?* Can you be corrected? If you can't, then get ready for a life of mistakes. *Correction Always Precedes Promotion!* This key is the most important one. If you are unteachable, then learning will become your greatest handicap. You can't help someone who knows it all. *Fruit* is the harvest reaped from a teachable life. In fact, we are commanded by God to bear fruit, and we are to be judged according to our fruit. The measuring stick of productivity is the **Fruit of the Spirit:** *"...love, peace, longsuffering, gentleness, goodness, faith, meekness, temperance: against such there is no law"* (Galatians 5:22). God requires fruit at three levels: First, you must bear fruit; second, you must bear more fruit; finally, you must bear much fruit. Your fruit *validates* a teachable heart. Fruit is not optional!

*"Every branch in me that **beareth not fruit he taketh away:** and every branch that beareth fruit, he purgeth it, that it may bring forth more fruit"* (John 15:2).

Growth is a progressive process, and growth comes through your willingness to learn. *How willing are you to learn?* It's your choice which method you'll use for growth. You can choose to grow the easier way which is through wisdom. Or you can grow the hard way which comes through experience. *It's your choice!* You see, if you're unwilling to learn through wisdom, then God has to use experience as your teacher. Why does He do this? Because He requires fruit, and He corrects whom he loves. So, welcome to the family! *Experience is a good teacher; however, it is a tardy one.* ~**Todd Coontz**

THREE THINGS THAT I MUST DO TO BECOME TEACHABLE

1. I must surrender my stubbornness.

*"For rebellion is as the sin of witchcraft, and **stubbornness** is as iniquity and idolatry..."*

1 Samuel 15:23

One day while I was driving down the road the Holy Spirit spoke to me and said, "Todd, I have never scheduled any of your defeats." I responded with, "What do You mean, You've never scheduled any of my defeats...then why have I suffered through so many?" God simply said, *"Todd, your stubbornness scheduled all of your defeats!"* Then I began to think about all the pain that I've suffered that could have been avoided if only I were teachable. My *stubbornness* created *pain...penalties...*and *regrets* for me. I almost became sick. If I only would have listened to the voice of the Holy Spirit my past could have been much easier. However, stubbornness demanded that I dig my heels into the ground and refuse to learn through wisdom. *What a fool I've been!* Still, God needed to get my attention and His character demanded fruit from my life. I left Him with no alternative. He now would have to teach me through *experience.*

What Is Stubbornness?

Stubbornness means: *to be unreasonably firm.* Here are several synonyms: contumacious, headstrong, inflexible, unyielding... just to name a few. *Are you stubborn?* If you are, then your future will be much harder than God ever planned it to be. Really, your stubbornness will take you down the road of hard knocks. In my early twenties just like so many young adults I thought I knew everything. I was very stubborn and unteachable. However, I possessed a heart for the things of God, and I wanted Him to accomplish good things with my life. God in His infinite love for me extended to me a hand of correction. I had many things going for me; however, my stubbornness held me back from promotion. *Correction always precedes promotion!* Yet how can someone who knows everything be corrected?

My attitude and unwillingness to learn set into motion a series of unfortunate events. These events would bring my life incredible pain and regret. Why? Because God required fruit from my life, and my life of self-will never yields the fruit of the Spirit. Fruit requires growth. And growth only comes from a teachable life. Growth comes in stages and is progressive. There will always be a season of cutting back so you will become more productive — *fruit...more fruit...much fruit.* I've already chronicled the painful events I faced in a previous chapter. As I have documented, my life has not always been a teachable one. Yet because I possessed a heart for God, He turned every experience into a lesson to teach me more about Him. God has instilled in everyone a right and wrong, and He's given us the ability to choose our path. God's great plan for each of us is to teach us through His wisdom, helping us to avoid our mistakes. However, if you disregard the wisdom of God as I did, you too will learn the harder way... through *experience*.

2. I must submit to authority.

*"**Submit** yourselves therefore to God. Resist the devil, and he will flee from you"* (James 4:7).

Submission means: *the act of yielding...humble behavior...obedient.* The learning process requires the act of submitting. Why? Another man's wisdom requires acceptance on your part that what he's teaching you is correct. This requires a submissive heart. It's easy to submit to someone when you agree with them. How do you respond when you don't agree? It's much harder, isn't it?

Why is submission so important? Because it relates to how we respond to God's authority. God's kingdom has been established by principles and laws. The authority of the believer is founded on God's law concerning *spiritual* authority. We have no authority other than what God has given to us. The entire Bible is about relating to authority. So it is reasonable to assume that God requires everything to submit under authority. This is God's highest law; and it transcends all others. The universe operates under this law; without it there would be total chaos.

✓ Nature is subject to time and seasons
✓ The earth rotates under the law of gravity
✓ Airplanes operate under the law of aerodynamics
✓ The animal kingdom submits to the lion

✓ Animals submit to man
✓ Children submit to their parents
✓ Man submits to government and employer
✓ *Everything submits to God*

Everything must submit. Your greatest discoveries will come through the *a*ct of submitting. Your most significant rewards will be the result of your willingness to submit. Society fights this with everything! We are told that submission is for the weak. Why? Because it's human nature to be rebellious. You can't even receive salvation without first submitting to God's plan of salvation. Anything you receive from God requires the act of submission. The word "submission" is not a bad word. It's your safety net out of danger! It's your protection against a life of self. It's the golden key to everything that God has promised you in His Word! *It's An Act Of Your Will.* What will you decide? Does this mean that every time you submit under authority nothing will ever go wrong? *No.* However, more things will certainly go right. Besides, God commands us to submit. *So how can you go wrong obeying God?*

*"Let every soul be **subject** unto the higher powers. For there is no power but of God: the powers that are **ordained** of God"* (Romans 13:1).

3. I must refuse to accept a spirit of offense.

"...It is impossible but that offenses will come: but woe unto him, through whom they come!" (Luke 17:1).

What is a "spirit of offense"? Webster's Dictionary defines offense: *resentment, an affront, an injustice, a misdemeanor, or attack.* An offense is simply Satan's tool to hold you back from becoming what God has called you to be. Correction always precedes promotion. God will allow people to come into your life for the purpose of correction. Yet if you're unteachable then you will never accept correction. Right? It's reasonable to assume, then, that you will remain in your present condition. We've learned the importance of information and how it's key to your belief system. You can only act on what you believe. Yet, if you will not receive from them, this information will never be woven in the fabric of your belief system. Consequently, you will remain *exactly* the way you are. What happens many times is when you are corrected, given advice, or simply supplied with new information you take offense. You take it too personal and perceive it to be an attack at your life.

A "CLOSED SPIRIT"

Have you ever had your feelings hurt by someone? I have. Do you believe that most people intentionally do this? Some... but not most. It's unintentional the majority of the time, and normally it's because they wanted their own way. Yet, if we take it personal, we will then "close our spirit" to the person who hurt us. What happens when you shut down emotionally?

Wrong things. You are then robbed of all the *information ...experiences... and wisdom* this person possesses. Why? Because you took what they said too personal. In addition, when this person recognizes how you responded, they will cease from offering help the second time. Because they really don't want to hurt your feelings. Who really suffers here? *You.*

THE GREEK WORD...*SKANDALON*

The Greek word for *offense* is **skandalon.** Our English word *scandalize* derives from this word. It refers to the part of the trap to which the bait is attached to ensnare or entrap its prey. Satan's objective here is to entrap or ensnare you into an unteachable life. He brings an offense into your life that will cause you to have a "closed spirit." How does the devil accomplish this? The key to success here is to camouflage the trap so you become ensnared and accept an offense. You may say to yourself, I'll never fall for this; I'm much too smart. Really? You're probably already much too close to the trap now, or worse...you're in it!

WHAT THE DEVIL USES FOR BAIT

Television portrays Satan as an evil man dressed in a red suit with a pitchfork in his hand. If he really looked this way then picking him out of a crowd would be easy. If it were only that simple! Of course, we know it's not. Satan is cunning, deceptive and will utilize any methods necessary to destroy your life. *What does the devil use for bait?* It's not what...*it's who.* When God wants to promote you, He brings a person into your life. However, when the devil wants to destroy you, he brings a person into your life. ***God uses people...the devil does too!*** Nothing in life ever gets accomplished without people. Nobody ever reaches the top all by themselves. You will *always* need help from someone.

Thus, the "spirit of offense" will usually come through someone closest to you.

- ✓ Family member or friend
- ✓ Mentor or pastor
- ✓ Husband or wife
- ✓ Employer or co-worker

Anybody you trust or believe in can be bait to ensnare you into an offense. **For example:**

- ✓ Cain became offended by Abel (Genesis 4:5)
- ✓ Naaman was offended by Elisha (2 Kings 5:10-12)
- ✓ Absalom was offended by Amnon (2 Samuel 13:22)
- ✓ Barnabas was offended by Paul
- ✓ Michal, David's wife, was offended by him (2 Samuel 6:15)

HOW TO OVERCOME OFFENSES

When you've been corrected, instructed, insulted or deeply hurt by someone, human nature is to retaliate. Human nature says, *"Who do you think you are telling me this or that?"* Because you were hurt, human nature naturally endeavors to protect itself from more hurt or pain. So you dig out bunkers and hide, or you build walls around your life. Both are there for protection. It's man's natural tendency to run away from or hide from anything that creates pain. I remember one day while I was no more than six years old, I put my hand on a hot stove after my mother had instructed me not to. Guess what happened? I was burned! Nobody ever had to tell me not to touch a hot stove again! Why? Because I wasn't getting burned the second time. I learned my lesson the hard way...through experience. This is exactly what happens to many when they become offended by someone. Their spirit becomes closed and the natural man takes over and declares, *"You're not getting close to me anymore; you hurt me."* Sadly, this happens too often. This causes you to become unteachable and even seem like a recluse. Life doesn't have to be this way. You can overcome the "spirit of offense" and become very teachable, if you will decide to work at it. I know this is possible because as you've read in previous chapters this was a problem for me. Here are three principles that have helped me to become teachable.

1. The Principle of Self-Examination.

"Wherefore, my beloved, as ye have always obeyed, not as in my presence only, but now much more in my absence, work out your own salvation with fear and trembling" (Philippians 2:12).

Immediately following any correction in my life I ask myself this question: *"Are they right?"* It doesn't matter who it came from. I've learned to receive correction from anyone. Why? Because if I'm doing something wrong, I want to know about it. A good friend of mine the other day said to me, "Todd, I can learn from you, because I know that you're not a wimp." She was acknowledging that she recognized that I could follow as well as lead. Examine yourself on a daily basis...make it a habit. If someone offers correction, criticism, or friendly advice...ask yourself, *"Are they right?"* Only two things can happen: First, if they're right...you have an opportunity to correct something that's probably holding you back from a promotion. Second, if they're wrong... then move on and simply forget about it. Either way...*You're A Winner!*

2. The Principle of a Humble Heart.

*"The sacrifices of God are a broken spirit: **a broken and contrite heart**, O God, thou wilt not despise."*
Psalms 51:17

Pride stinks! If you want to fall hard, then exalt yourself. It has been said that *it's hard to fall when you're on your knees.*

*"**Pride goeth before destruction,** and a haughty spirit before a fall"* (Proverbs 16:18).

Nobody likes to be around an arrogant person, not even the arrogant. Pride is the root of so many problems today in society. Many don't even recognize pride when it's part of their character. What is pride? It's an exaggerated self-esteem. Pride will make you think of yourself as being something more than you really are. With pride it becomes easier to be offended because you believe you know more than the person who corrected you. Instead of asking yourself, "Are they right?" you will automatically assume that they're wrong. Don't allow pride to rob you of what God has for you!

3. The Principle of Forgiving.

*"And be ye kind one to another, tenderhearted, **for-giving one another,** even as God for Christ's sake hath forgiven you"* (Ephesians 4:32).

Jesus was very clear in seeing we understood the danger of harboring unforgiveness. He was very direct when speaking about this important subject. He illustrates through a parable the consequences of having an offense in your heart. We find it in Matthew 18:21-35. The scene starts with Peter asking a probing question:

*"Then came Peter to him, and said, Lord, how oft shall my brother sin against me, and I **forgive** him? till seven times?"* (Matthew 18:21).

Peter assumed that to forgive someone seven times was more than generous. This was a reasonable assumption on Peter's part; after all, seven was the number of completion. He must have thought to himself, *"How much forgiveness can a person expect you to give, anyway?"* Yet Jesus' response was very different than what Peter expected.

"...I say not unto thee, Until seven times: but, Until seventy times seven" (Matthew 18:22).

Wow! Did Jesus know what He was saying? You should forgive an *infinite* number of times. Who deserves such forgiveness! I can see Peter's face...what shock! You see, Peter was the kind of man who acted first, then asked questions later. In his mind he believed to forgive someone seven times was a stretch. Now Jesus was telling them that seven was not enough. Can you imagine what was going through their minds? Jesus saw their reaction. He witnessed their bewilderment. I believe that this was what triggered Jesus' teaching. He wanted to make certain they understood. Therefore, to clarify and answer all their questions, He began to teach them this parable.

There was a certain king who reckoned with his servants when he discovered one that owed him ten thousand talents. The king commanded that he and his family and everything he had be sold to pay their debt. This servant fell down and worshiped him, begging him for forgiveness. Compassion flooded the king's heart and he forgave him the entire debt.

Now, this same servant went out and found one of his fellow servants who owed him money...*a hundred pence*. He took him by the throat and demanded payment at once; however, the servant could not pay. Even though the servant begged his forgiveness, he would not forgive him and threw him into prison.

When the king discovered what had happened he was infuriated! He commanded the servant to be brought to him and, after questioning him, threw him into prison with the tormentors. After Jesus was finished with this teaching He closed with:

*"So likewise shall my heavenly Father **do also unto you**, if ye from your hearts forgive not every one his brother their trespasses"* (Matthew 18:35).

Jesus' message is very explicit concerning forgiveness...*we must forgive!* No matter how deep the hurt or offense, if we don't freely forgive, we will be turned over to the tormentors.

Why is it so important for you to forgive? Because forgiveness is a debt *you owe*. But when you forgive it cancels that debt. Look at the Lord's prayer:

*"For if you **forgive** men their trespasses, your heavenly Father will also forgive you"* (Matthew 6:14).

Forgiveness is your choice! Is there unforgiveness in your heart for someone today? Who has hurt you? Have you forgiven them? *You can.* Simply decide to forgive. Offenses will come, and things in life will go wrong. If you will allow God to cut back everything that's not producing fruit, if you will allow Him to teach you wisdom through a mentor and learn from their experience, you can move to the next level of promotion that God has for you! Don't allow Satan to ensnare or entrap you with an offense. Examine yourself by asking, "Are they right?" Humble yourself before God, and forgive those who hurt you. You will become teachable and will be rewarded for it!

KEY # 2...The Holy Spirit Is Your Governing Teacher.

*"But the Comforter, which is the Holy Ghost, whom the Father will send in my name, he shall **teach you all things,** and bring all things to your remembrance, whatsoever I have said to you"* (John 14:26).

It was a hot, humid, and muggy evening in July. It was the middle of summer in West Virginia and the year was 1977. A couple hundred church people were gathered around a stage in the middle of a cow pasture. It was getting dark, and was just dark enough to see the lightning bugs flickering in the night air. It was campmeeting time in the mountains. Excitement was in the air. People were gathering together from several churches in anticipation of a move of God! I had just given my life to Christ previously in February in that same year. God saved me, healed me, and called me, and I preached my first message — all at the tender age of ten. God had already done so much for me; however, little did I know how much more He wanted to give. My first mentor was Rev. Bud Marshall. This man spent countless hours with me teaching me about God. He introduced me to Jesus, and for the first ten years of my Christian walk he mentored me tirelessly. He was my Paul, and I was his Timothy. In fact, I've dedicated this book to him. One thing really sticks out in my mind about something he said to me: *"Todd, simply ask God for whatever you need and He will give it to you."* You know what? *I believed him.*

That night after the preacher had finished preaching his message, an altar call was given. People who needed prayer for salvation, healing, and the baptism in the Holy Spirit flooded the altar. I had already received my salvation and healing, but I had never been baptized in the Holy Spirit. God had already given me so much! Yet I wanted everything that He promised to give me. *I wanted all of Him!*

As I stepped out into the freshly mowed aisle, I began to make my way toward the altar. I pushed through the crowd until I reached the altar. I knelt down in prayer and remember telling God, *"I want everything You have to give to me, even the Holy Spirit."* I really didn't understand all that was happening that night. But I remember feeling such a calm and peace in my heart. After all, my life had been filled with such rejection and pain, this was a welcomed feeling. *Then it happened!* The preacher laid his hands on me and said, *"God, give him whatever he's asking for."* The next thing I knew, I was laid out on the ground speaking in other tongues. *Wow!* I had never felt this way before. God baptized me in the Holy Ghost! My life has never been the same again! **Note:** Some who may read this book will not agree with some of my teaching on the subject of tongues as it pertains to the Holy Spirit. I will not debate you concerning this, because I'm sure about what I believe about this most important topic. I know what God did for me, and my life was radically changed that night through this experience. Today, I'm in love with the Person of the Holy Spirit... *He is God!*

The Holy Spirit is your primary teacher. He is not wind, fire, or a white dove.

He is not an "it."
He is a Person.
He is God.

Jesus recognized Him as our primary teacher or mentor.

*"...He shall **teach you all things,** and bring all things to your remembrance..."* (John 14:26).

The *Holy Spirit* can enter your life like:

Fire to purify you (Acts 2:3,4)
Water to refresh you (Isa. 44:3,4)
Wind moving swiftly and suddenly (Act 2:2)

He is a *Person,* not merely a presence, or an atmosphere, attitude, or even the environment. My life changed the day I met Him! Allow Him to *teach, correct,* and *instruct* your life. He can help you avoid the pain through mistakes. He is omniscient, omnipotent, and omnipresent. He is more than ready to teach you "all things"! *Will you allow Him to today?*

THE GREATEST *DISCOVERY* OF MY LIFE!

The greatest loss in the Garden of Eden was not the loss of authority, dominion, or possession. The *greatest* loss was *the loss of His Presence!* God walked with man in the cool of the evening. Think about that! Sin entered the heart of man and stripped him of man's greatest gift...access to God's Presence! That's why God hates sin so much! Because sin cannot enter His presence. *God is Holy!* Sin robs God of His greatest pleasure...fellowship with His creation. He created man for relationship, and breathed into man...*His life.* He created you in His image and likeness. You are His greatest accomplishment, and He loves communion with you. Yet sin can steal all of this from God. Is there sin in your life today? God will forgive you if only you will ask.

*"If we **confess** our sins, he is faithful and just to **forgive us** our sins, and to **cleanse** us from all unrighteousness"* (1 John 1:9).

The greatest discovery of my life is: *God Never Turns Away A Seeking Heart!* If you haven't found Him, then you're simply not seeking Him with all of your heart. He promises that if we will seek Him with everything that's in us, we will find Him.

*"I love them that **love me**; and those that **seek me** early shall **find me**"* (Proverbs 8:17).

*"For every one that asketh receiveth; and he that **seeketh findeth**; and to him that knocketh it shall be opened"* (Luke 11:10).

God Never Turns Away A Seeking Heart! Ask Him today for more...He will give it! Seek Him for His wisdom...you will get it! *Open* your heart to receive from Him...and you will receive it! Remember, your primary teacher is the Person of the Holy Spirit. He will help you to become more like Jesus.

- ⇨ He Will *Develop* Your Character.
- ⇨ He Will *Remind* You What He Taught You.
- ⇨ He Will *Guide* You Through Your Storms.
- ⇨ He Will *Comfort* You In Pain.
- ⇨ He Will *Speak* Of Things To Come.
- ⇨ He Will Always *Lift Up* Jesus.
- ⇨ He Is Not Merely A Presence...*He Is A Person!* Receive Him Today!

KEY # 3...You Can Learn By
Mentors Or Mistakes.

"He that walketh with wise men shall be wise: but a companion of fools shall be destroyed."

Proverbs 13:20

The Holy Spirit is your primary teacher. However, He will bring a variety of people into your life to teach you. Always confirm what you've been taught by others with the Word of God and the your inner peace. Peace is chief! Another way to avoid mistakes is to learn through mentors. Mentors can teach you, through their experiences and wisdom, lessons they learned the hard way. *What is a mentor?* Mentors are trusted teachers. I have been fortunate to have had several trusted teachers in my life. Today, my success is a collection of their combined wisdom in my life. They have corrected me, instructed me, encouraged me, and loved me to success! The greatest learning in my life has taken place at the feet of a mentor. Without them in my life, my life would be less, not more.

Dr. Mike Murdock is one of my closest friends and mentors. The lessons I've learned from him have radically changed my life. His wisdom has challenged me to become more. Recently I received his *Wisdom Commentary* on 52 different topics. If you haven't received one, you need to get one for your library. I want you to see some things that he teaches about *An Uncommon Mentor* in chapter 30. *An Uncommon Mentor Is Not Necessarily Your Best Friend.*

📖 Your best friend loves you *the way you are.* Your mentor loves you *too much to leave you the way you are.*

📖 Your best friend is comfortable with your *past.* Your mentor is comfortable with your *future.*

📖 Your best friend *ignores* your weakness. Your mentor *removes* your weakness.

📖 Your best friend is your *cheerleader.* Your mentor is your *coach...* Mentors are more than your best friend; they are your *trusted teacher.*

KEY # 4...You Must Be Willing To *Invest* In Learning.

*"For which of you, intending to build a tower, sitteth not down first, and **counteth the cost,** whether he have sufficient to finish it"* (Luke 14:28).

L earning is costly! It will cost you...*time...money...and trust.* They tell me that the average four year college education costs more than $12,000 a year. That's only in *monetary* terms. How much *time* will it cost? Education is costly! You can learn through mentors. They are worth more than what we pay for higher education. They can teach us lessons they learned the *hard* way. They can help you to avoid their past mistakes.

1. It will cost you time... Why? Because you're on *his time schedule, not yours.* I have the rare opportunity of traveling at least twice a month with Dr. Mike Murdock. I never ask him to change his schedule to accommodate me. Why? Because I'm there to learn from him.

Always remember this: *The Person Who Has More To Receive Always Abides By The Schedule Of The Person Who Has More To Give!* ~**Todd Coontz**

2. It will cost you money... *Why? Because I don't want what's in his hand; I want what's in his heart.* Traveling isn't cheap! Airfare...gas...hotels...food...taxicabs all cost money. Books... tapes...and study materials all cost money. Your mentor also qualifies for your seed. I sow on a regular basis into the life of my mentors. You should too! My pastor is one of my mentors and I sow into his life on a regular basis. Why? Because he invests in my life through his wisdom and love. Also, because I respect the way he follows after God's heart.

3. It will cost you trust... *Why? Because to receive loyalty you must show loyalty.* Your mentor is your trusted teacher. If you're going to learn from him, then you must *trust* him. It goes much further than trust. You must be *loyal* to him. What is loyalty? Webster says: fidelity in duty. Webster's Thesaurus: allegiance; devotion; obedience. Don't confuse loyalty with faithfulness. Faithfulness is consistency. *Loyalty is exclusive.*

KEY # 5...You Must Ask For Correction.

"Give instruction to a wise man, and he will be yet wiser: teach a just man, and he will increase in learning" (Proverbs 9:9).

*A*sk *for correction?* You may be thinking, "Isn't he supposed to know this in the first place? *Yes.* But many *proteges* don't receive correction very well. In fact, when most are corrected they become "offended" and close their heart. It's virtually impossible to be mentored without a teachable spirit.

How do you ask your mentor to correct you? First, you simply ask. Tell him verbally, "Sir, you have my permission to correct me." Second, by your attitude. After he corrects you, how do you respond? Your attitude will indicate whether or not you qualify for more of his wisdom. If you continually argue with him, or offer excuses, he'll see this, and you will eventually lose access to his wisdom. This doesn't mean that correction won't sometimes hurt, or even cause you to want to defend yourself. This is a natural human reaction; however, you must crucify your flesh and ask yourself, *"Is he right?"* Remember, he has nothing to gain from correcting you. Yet he has everything to lose; however, he loves you too much to allow you to remain unchanged! Third, your willingness to return is a good indication that you're teachable and growing. Simply say, *"Thank you* for loving me enough to correct me. I know you're only trying to help me."

Finally, Remind...Reward...Review...and Return. REMIND him that you appreciate his time and wisdom. *REWARD* him through gifts and money. *REVIEW* with him his last instructions and let him know the actions you're taking to correct them. RETURN every moment he gives you with your time to help him achieve his goals...dreams...desires.

How I Learned To FOCUS

"...but, this one thing I do..."
Philippians 3:13

CHAPTER 7

*F*ocus means...*a concentrated effort.* Paul declared, "...this *one* thing...," not many things, but *one* thing I do! Here is where we miss it. Rarely does anything receive our total focus. If the devil can divide your *focus* he can sabotage your dreams, hopes, and desires. Your ability to focus determines your success! **Thomas Edison,** the great inventor, was asked, *"Why are you more successful than your peers?"* He replied, "It's quite simple...others think about many things all day long, but I think about only *one* thing all day long." **Charles Dickens** once said, "I never could have done without the habits of punctuality, order and diligence...The determination to concentrate myself on *one* subject at a time."

There are no magic formulas or secret ingredients. The key to unlocking doors of opportunity and achieving what you want in life is simply focus. The problem most people face is that they are focusing on the wrong things. For example, someone who lives from paycheck to paycheck each week might spend their time focusing on their lack of money. They will complain about never having quite enough to live, instead of focusing on how to acquire the skills for a better job. Many people are stuck in a job or career they find boring and unfulfilling because they have not focused on developing their area of expertise.

I recently read that race car drivers never look at the wall. Why? Because their *focus* needs to be on the road...not the wall. *Your Mind Gravitates In The Direction Your Eyes Are Focused.*

⇨ Adam and Eve *saw* the fruit.
⇨ Jeremiah *saw* the potter working with the clay.
⇨ Isaiah *saw* the Lord high and lifted up.
⇨ Peter *saw* the waves crashing against his legs.
⇨ Jesus *saw* the crowds.
⇨ Your eyes are a window. To produce different results you must change what you're *seeing*.

To help you remember the importance of focusing, I'm going to use the word *FOCUS* as an acronym. Each of these five keys that will help you unlock every door that is presently closed. **F**ind...**O**mit...**C**reate...**U**nderstand...**S**eize: they equal...**FOCUS!**

FOCUS KEY # 1

F*ind* A Pen And List The Six Most Important Goals That You Need To Complete Today.

"...Write the vision, and make it plain upon tables, that he may run that readeth it" (Habakkuk 2:2).

F**ocus requires a concentrated effort.** Someone once said, *"A short pencil is better than a long memory."* You cannot concentrate unless there's clarity in your goal setting. *Writing creates clarity.* When you commit something to paper it helps you to think more clearly. For example, you are not reading the *original* manuscript of this book. It has been written and rewritten a dozen times. Why? *For clarity.* Each time becoming more clear and precise on each topic discussed. Writing also helps *clear* your mind for creativity. Your greatest tool for ideas, solutions, and provocative thought is your mind. When you write down the things you need to remember it untangles your mind to focus, thereby providing you with ideas, solutions, and provocative thought.

Mary Kay Ash, founder of Mary Kay Cosmetics, would write down six things to do as a daily habit. She would prioritize them from most important to least important, and one by one she would complete each task. Writing her goals down helped her become more focused on what she needed to do that day. What do you need to focus on today? What requires your immediate attention? Establish your goals. Write them down. List them from the most important one to the least important one, and passionately accomplish them one by one. This will help you determine what is *expedient* and what is *expendable.* This is a daily habit for me. This habit alone has helped me accomplish more than any other habit I have. *Try it.*

FOCUS KEY # 2

O*mit* **Distractions From Your Life.**

*"For God is not the **author** of confusion, but of peace..."* (1 Corinthians 14:33).

Focus brings clarity and peace. Broken focus brings confusion and strife. Anything that hinders you from completing your task is a distraction. To bring *clarity* and *peace* back into your life you have to identify and determine the appropriate actions to take. For example, sometimes while I'm writing in my study at home, our dog starts barking and she will not stop. This is distracting and hinders me from clear thought, which makes it more difficult to write. I have to decide the appropriate course of action to take in order to resolve this distraction. Since I love our dog, and her affection means more to me than her barking, I simply find another room in which to write. In contrast, it's impossible for me to write at my office, so I do all of my writing at home. It's up to you to decide what problems can be solved simply, and which ones require more evasive actions. What distracts you? What keeps you from focusing? *Identify* it. Take appropriate action. *Remove it!*

FOCUS KEY # 3

Create An Environment That Makes You Productive.

*"And when he had sent the multitudes away, he went up into a **mountain** apart to pray..."* (Matthew 14:23).

Environment matters. Where you are is as important as what you are. Airplanes need the sky. Ships need the water. Cars need the road. The environment you create will determine the level of productivity you can give to any task. What environment motivates you to be more productive? What things can you surround yourself with to motivate you? Who motivates you? When you become motivated you will have the persistence to become focused. *Your Motivation Will Determine Your Focus!* I like an atmosphere that is quiet and peaceful. I am also motivated by pictures. I like to see what I'm believing for or dreaming about. So I hang pictures around my study. For example, the covers to all my books that I'm currently writing are completed long before I write them. Why? Because seeing the ending motivates me to complete the beginning. Many writers will complete the final chapter of a book before they have started with the first chapter. I also have a picture of my new airplane I'm praying for. Pictures of my wife and son sit on my desk, along with a picture of my parents. Why? Because I want to remind myself of what God has done and is going to do for me. I also love water and a manicured yard. At any time I can walk over to my window in my office and see water running and a putting green in my backyard. *They motivate me to complete!* Find what *excites* you. Create an environment that will permit you to be happy and productive. *Happy People Are Productive People!*

FOCUS KEY # 4

Understand Your Purpose And Gifts In Life.

*"A man's **gift** maketh room for him, and bringeth him before great men"* (Proverbs 18:16).

Everyone has a purpose in life. God has given every person gifts. You must *discover* and *focus* on what your purpose and gifts are. Your discovery will come through questions. What have you been gifted to do? What are you passionate about? What do you hate? What do you love? What comes natural to you? *Your Purpose Is Your Discovery!* Here are three clues to discovering your purpose and gifts. You discover your purpose by: 1) What You Hate; 2) What You Love; 3) What Comes Natural To You.

THREE CLUES TO DISCOVERING YOUR PURPOSE AND GIFTS

1. You Discover Your Purpose By What You Hate.

What do you hate? Your anger can motivate you to take action against what you hate. *I hate poverty!* My hatred for poverty motivates me and keeps me traveling thousands of miles and scheduling hundreds of appointments each year. I want to help people fulfill their dreams by solving their financial problems. My hatred for poverty keeps me focused on the solutions to each financial problem. *What You Hate Will Determine What You Are Willing To Attack!* Discover and focus your hate on the right things. *Your Purpose Can Be Discovered Through Anger.*

2. You Discover Your Purpose By What You Love.

What do you love? What excites you the most? What would you do for free? Love is a powerful emotion. The Bible says that all else may fail, but love will never fail. Tiger Woods loves golf. Jeff Gordon loves racing. Thomas Kinkade loves to paint. Donald Trump loves real estate. Bill Gates loves computers. Your love is a good indication of something you can be passionate about. *Your Purpose Is Hidden In What You Love.*

3. You Discover Your Purpose By What Comes Natural.

This discovery is perhaps the most important of them all. It is possible to love something and be horrible at it. America's favorite sport is said to be baseball. I know a lot of people who are in love with the game. Some even grew up believing that someday they would be in the Major League. So even though your love for something is there, it doesn't guarantee you are any good at it.

For example, Michael Jordan is an all-star basketball player, arguably the greatest to have ever played the game. Michael loves the game of basketball and it comes natural to him. He loves baseball as well. He worked very hard to become a great baseball player and made tremendous sacrifices because of his love for the game. Although he worked hard and focused his energy on becoming a good player, it did not appear he had the same *natural* talent for baseball as he did for basketball. Whatever comes natural to you is a good indication of something you are gifted to do. Love or hate is not enough to guarantee success. But couple them with your natural gifts and your purpose will emerge! *Your Purpose Is Your Discovery Of What Comes Natural.* Understand what it is, what it may cost, how much time will be involved, and pursue it! Your focus will be more deliberate when you discover your purpose. Through this discovery your gifts will emerge. You have a purpose. *Discover what it is!*

FOCUS KEY # 5

Seize Every Moment As An Opportunity To Focus.

*"See then that ye walk circumspectly, not as fools, but as wise, Redeeming the **time** for the days are evil."*
Ephesians 5:15, 16

HERE ARE SEVEN KEYS TO *REDEEMING* THE TIME.

Key # 1. Invest your time instead of spending it.

You measure time in seconds, minutes, and hours. There is only so much sand in the hourglass. Who gets it? You must decide. *Make Every Moment Count!* Everyone has been given an equal amount of time in a day. So use your time wisely. Listen to tapes on your way to work. Buy a recorder to document what you need to get completed for that day. Waiting at the doctor's office is an opportunity to read a book that will educate you on how to reach your daily goals.

Key # 2. Remove, turn off,
or avoid things that rob your time.

*E*xcessive TV watching is a time waster. It's alarming how much time is wasted lying in front of the TV with a remote control in one hand and a sandwich in the other. The only exercise some people get is channel surfing. *(Smile)* A study by Nielsen Company, which specializes in recording how many people watch TV, what they watch and how often they watch, offers these statistics. On average, people watch TV *6.5 hours* per day. At this rate, in an average life span you would spend about *eleven years* of your life watching TV! By the way, if you just stopped watching the commercials, you'd save about three years. What would happen if you decided to slash your TV watching in half? You would add about *forty-eight days* to your productivity. This would be equal to nearly *two months* of quality time to pursue more worthwhile endeavors. *Consider this.*

*T*he telephone is perhaps the most insidious time waster of all. It always amazes me how people allow a little piece of hardware to control their day. If you are needing to get something urgent completed, unplug the phone. And turn off your cellular or any other device that may distract you. Voice mail, e-mail, and answering machines can help you avoid these interruptions. Obviously there are times when you need to be available, so pre-schedule your appointments and set aside time to make needed phone calls. Please do not allow gadgets to control your day! These devices can help you become more productive and manage your valuable time if used efficiently.

*P*eople may attempt to rob your time. They may call you just to chat awhile, not realizing you're attempting to complete something important. Sometimes they may wander in your office for a chat because you have an open door policy. They may even see you at the local grocery store and use that time to catch up. What happens to me sometimes is while I'm mowing the grass someone will stop me to talk or ask me questions. I call them *time-robbers*. They are normally fine, good intentioned people who don't mean any harm. They have probably finished their work for the day. You have to politely excuse yourself and communicate to them that you have several must-be-done-today things to complete. They will normally understand.

Key # 3.   Establish short and long term goals.

If you don't have a set of established goals for the day, goals that will take you from point A to point B, you will begin to mistake *activity* for *accomplishment.* Establish 24 hour, 7 day, 30 day, 6 month, 1, 3 and 5 year goals. The Japanese have 100 year goals.

Key # 4.   Set a timetable for completion.

Don't spend an hour doing a 20-minute job! When you establish a *time frame* you become more aware of how much time you have for a specific task. There is a difference in being busy and taking specific, well-planned action. Without a plan your day will evaporate and your goals will go unfinished. Also, when you establish a time frame don't only set them according to a task, but also for activities within a task.

Key # 5. Delegate things to someone else.

Spend your time being productive in the areas you're passionate about, have a gift for, or will produce your greatest reward. For example, I love to mow grass. I enjoy the fresh smell of newly cut grass. Also, it allows me to get badly needed exercise. But when I have more pressing things to do (like complete this book) I hire someone else to mow for me. You always weigh the rewards and benefits of every task or goal. If you don't, there will always be something else less pressing waiting to rob your valuable time.

Key # 6. Schedule your most important tasks when your energy is at its highest level.

When is your energy level at peak performance? Is it first thing in the morning? Maybe it's midday. How about late evening? Everyone has a *time* during their day when they're at peak performance. You must identify when that is and do the most difficult and mentally challenging tasks during this time. It is difficult to work on "must be done today things" when your energy level is headed south. Your focus will be at its highest level when you...*Identify*...*Determine*...and *Schedule* each task accordingly!

Key # 7. Learn to use the latest time-saving technologies.

We're living in a technological society today. The information highway has revolutionized the way we're planning our daily lives. Your personal pocket computer, e-mail, cellular phones, pagers, and computers are only a few devices that can help you manage your time more efficiently. Initially, they will require an investment of your time to learn how to operate them. However, the future time saved will far outweigh the present time invested. Also, take the time to learn how to use them properly. *Your Focus Will Determine Your Future!*

Find...**O**mit...**C**reate...**U**nderstand...*and* **S**eize *every opportunity to focus on what God has promised to you!*

Together they all add up to...FOCUS!

7 Things I Will Do To Focus

1.

2.

3.

4.

5.

6.

7.

Please, Don't Repo My Car

*"But thou shalt remember the Lord thy God: for it is he that giveth thee **power** to get wealth, that he may **establish** [confirm] his **covenant** which he sware unto thy fathers, as it is this day."*

Deuteronomy 8:18

CHAPTER 8

*I*t was early spring. It was a beautiful, star-filled Friday night in 1989. It was approximately 11:00 pm when I returned home to my small apartment. I had just settled down for the night when I heard a knock at my door. I was startled at first because it was late, and I wasn't sure who could be knocking at my door at such a late hour. I jumped out of the bed and got dressed and went to the door to see who it was. While I was looking through the peephole I asked them, "Who are you and what do you want?" They simply replied, "We need to talk to you for a moment." I said, "What about?" Then I heard the most heart-wrenching statement: *"You're behind three payments on your car and we're here to get it!"* I thought to myself, they're here to *repo* my car. I can't believe this is happening to me — after all, I'm a child of God! I finally opened the door and stepped outside to talk to them. They asked me for the keys and I refused, and I told them that I would talk to my banker tomorrow morning to straighten this out. They reluctantly agreed to wait, and said they would be back the next day. Somehow I was able to work something out with the bank the next day. I was glad that my car was never repossessed.

FINANCIAL STRESS IS DEVASTATING!

*E*veryone faces financial stress sometime in their life. It is a time when things seem hopeless. A time when all seems lost. When every day becomes a day filled with the same ritual as the day before. Even the simple act of getting up out of the bed in the morning presents a challenge. You know what is waiting for you right down the hall...yesterday's struggle. A day filled with a mountain of unpaid bills, debts, and a ringing phone that never stops because of nagging bill collectors. It can become overwhelming at best! There is nothing more stressful than financial worry. It can cause even the strongest stomach to feel sick. It will zap you of the energy you once possessed. It will cause you to think irrationally. It will steal your peace and rob your sleep. *Financial stress is devastating!* We must not forget that God wants us to be free from financial worry.

> *"The thief cometh not, but for to steal, and to kill, and to destroy: I am come that they might have **life**, and that they might have it **more abundantly.**"*
>
> John 10:10

I WAS PUZZLED BECAUSE
I DIDN'T UNDERSTAND... *WHY?*

What I'm about to share with you took me years to discover for myself. If you will listen and hear with your heart, it will explain why many good-hearted Christians are broke. As you recall, when they came to repossess my car I was puzzled because I didn't understand why God would allow this to happen to me. After all, I was a preacher. Many were being saved, set free, and healed in my meetings. Yet my finances were a wreck! Why? Simply put, being a good person *only* doesn't qualify you for money. If being good was the only qualification for money, then why did Mother Teresa die broke? Was she not a good person? What about all the innocent children around the world who are dying because they have no money for food? Think about it for a moment. How many people do you know who are good human beings, who subsequently are struggling financially? *Many.*

In contrast, being bad doesn't disqualify you from having money. If being bad excluded you from having money, then why isn't the mob broke? Do you know anyone who seems to be inherently evil who has money? *Sure.* I have discovered two things concerning money that has literally changed my life. First, being good or bad has nothing to do with attracting money. Second, money itself is neither good nor bad. Money is neutral, and it takes on the personality and character of the person who possesses it. If you want more money than you have now then you must *qualify* for it. Many have become disillusioned about God's willingness to provide for His children. Some will go as far as to say that poverty is a virtue, and the more impoverished you are the more spiritual you become. The reason that many believe this way is that they don't understand the true Biblical message of prosperity. They have also believed that being good alone qualified them for financial increase, or they have simply not been taught *how* to qualify for money.

THE BIBLE HAS TWO SIDES
COVERING DIFFERENT TOPICS

I learned this from my mentor and good friend, Dr. Mike Murdock. The Bible has two sides: 1) *The Person of Jesus*; 2) *The Principles of Jesus*. The Person of Jesus gets you ready for *heaven*, while His principles get you prepared for *earth*. The Person of Jesus brings you your *peace*, while His principles bring your *prosperity*. It is possible to be ready for heaven, yet not prepared for earth. The thief next to Jesus on the cross proves this. In a *moment* Jesus forgave him and declared to him..."Today you will be with me in paradise." However, even though he was ready for heaven in a moment, it takes a lifetime to equip yourself for a successful life on earth. The Church has embraced the *Person* of Jesus while rejecting His financial principles and has plummeted into poverty! The world has embraced the *principles* of Jesus while rejecting the Person and has prospered! Why? Because there are two sides to the Gospel. Knowing Jesus is only the beginning. You must also know His Word!

*"Then said Jesus to those Jews which believed on him, If you **continue in my word**, then are you my **disciples** indeed; And you shall **know** the truth, and the **truth** shall make you free"* (John 8:31-32).

THE DAY MY LIFE CHANGED FINANCIALLY

It was the month of September 1990. The temperature in South Carolina was becoming cooler. Fall was finally here! This time of the year is always my favorite season. I remember sitting one day in my small two bedroom apartment staring at all of the unpaid bills and thinking, *"There has got to be a better way!"* I was fed up! I was tired of struggling financially and never having quite enough money to pay everything. Many of you know exactly what I'm talking about. I had tried everything ...I recalculated my income versus my expenses...I looked for ways to cut back...I even tried using a different method of calculating. It was like hitting my head against a brick wall. Still, no matter which way I looked at it, I always fell short of what I needed to pay everything. I was swimming in a muddled financial cesspool...I felt like I was drowning! I didn't understand why God would allow me to go through something that brought me so much pain. I was frustrated, discouraged, hurt, and mad...all at the same time! Worst of all, there really didn't seem to be a light at the end of the tunnel, or any pot of gold on the other side of the rainbow. *I felt hopeless!*

Then it happened! I heard a still, small voice speaking to me. It was the voice of the Holy Spirit. I knew His voice. He spoke to me often. Ever since I was just a little boy I had developed a heart for the voice of God. So I quietly listened to what He wanted to say to me: *"Todd, are you tithing and giving like I said to do in my Word?"* Well, I knew the answer to that. *No.* Really, this wasn't what I wanted to hear. Of course, I had a long list of excuses as to why I was not tithing and giving any of my money to God. So I rattled them off one by one until I had whittled them down to just one. And I really felt like I had offered quite a defensive argument to Him. *"Lord, I can't afford to. When I get more money I will give. You don't need my money."* I concluded with, *"I need it more than You do!"* After I had exhausted my list and pleaded my case with God, He simply said to me, *"To get what I have, you have to do what I say."* I knew exactly what He wanted me to do, and even knew where to find all of the scriptures. Many of them I had even memorized! Finally, through my frustration and discouragement... I surrendered to His will.

The day my life changed financially wasn't when I could afford to purchase a $70,000 luxury car. Neither was it the day I moved into a million dollar gated community into a new 5,000-square-foot house with a pool in the backyard and a guest house. These things represent financial milestones in my life; however, achieving them wasn't the day my life changed forever.

By the world's standards I have achieved success! Yet none of these material possessions or achievements contributed initially to changing my life. My life changed forever financially... *the day I changed my mind about giving!* When I decided to obey God's Word about the law of sowing and reaping...that day my life changed!

> *"Will a man **rob** God? Yet ye have robbed me. But ye say, Wherein have we robbed thee? In **tithes** and **offerings**. Ye are cursed with a curse: for ye have robbed me, even this whole nation"* (Malachi 3:8-9).

"God, I'm Going To Do It Your Way..."

It has been said, "When you get to the end of your rope, tie a knot and hang on!" Finally, I came to the end of my rope, and that's exactly what I did! As I sat in my small two bedroom apartment assessing my current financial condition, I came to resolve...I needed to change. So I did. I began my journey of change through making a real commitment to God about the Biblical issue of tithing. I promised Him to start tithing faithfully and said, "God, I'm going to do it Your way. But if it doesn't work then I don't really want to serve a God who doesn't provide my needs." I was sincere and very honest with God. Someone might say, "Who do you think you are talking to God that way?" or "You can't threaten God like that." God knew my heart. He knew that my statement wasn't a sign of disrespect; it was a statement of *faith!*

One of my greatest discoveries of my lifetime about God is: *God Doesn't Respond To My Needs: He Only Responds To My Faith!* If God was *need* motivated then all of the hungry children in Africa would be fed. Every hospital in the world would become vacant immediately. God is not *Need* Responsive. *He is Faith Oriented!* This truth alone seems to be the very essence of God's very existence.

> *"But without faith it is impossible to please him: for he that cometh to God must **believe** that he is, and that he is a **rewarder** of them that diligently seek him."*
> Hebrews 11:6

YOU DON'T HAVE TO BE A *ROCKET SCIENTIST*

When I made my commitment to God to start tithing a portion of what I earned, my income was very minuscule. I was making $200 each week...before taxes. My apartment rent was $550 each month, and my utilities were approximately $150. I had a car payment of $341.89 and my car insurance was $250 each month. In addition, I had to buy gas, food, pay my debts, pay insurance premiums, and still have enough money left over for miscellaneous items. My bills could easily total more than $1,500 each month. My problem was that my income was only $800 a month. Now, you don't have to be a "rocket scientist" to do the math here!

Now you know why they were coming to repossess my car. Just to mention, I have also had my electricity shut off, my water turned off, and my phone disconnected during these days of financial lack. I know how it feels to be hungry and have no money for food. I understand what it's like to "borrow" money for gas to get to work. Even now as I remember the way things used to be, I still feel the sting of financial torment and the pain of poverty. *I hate poverty!* It's not God's perfect will for you to suffer lack!

> *"Beloved, I wish **above all things** [every aspect] that thou mayest **prosper** and be in health, even as thy soul prospereth"* (John 3:2).

I WRECKED AND TOTALED MY CAR

Less than one month after I decided to start tithing to God, I wrecked my car. It was totaled; at least now they had nothing to repossess. *(Smile)* Every step in the direction of God causes a struggle between you and the devil. The devil isn't going to just sit around while you reach for God's financial promises. We are engaged in a *spiritual battle* against the devil.

"For we wrestle not against flesh and blood, but against principalities, against powers, against the rulers of the darkness of this world, against **spiritual wickedness** *in high places"* (Ephesians 6:10).

Many never experience true financial freedom because they never learn to stand firm on God's Word. Paul writes these words of encouragement to the Corinthian church.

"Therefore, my beloved brethren, be ye **steadfast**, *unmovable, always abounding in the work of the Lord..."*
1 Corinthians 15:58

Anytime you decide to accept God at His Word...there will always be confrontation from the devil! The most severe confrontation will always come after your first steps of faith, because he knows that your first steps are generally the most difficult ones to take. Why? Because human nature responds to circumstances based on the natural realm of things. It is natural for you to say, "I will believe it after I see it." However, God says, *"Believe it and then you will see it."* The devil knows that God responds only to faith. When you're obedient to God's Word...it's a *Step of Faith.*

Take Note: *His Written Word Always Parallels His Spoken Word!*

The reason why so many collapse under the pressures of struggle is because when the devil strikes, most Christians tend to rely on the natural realm, instead of God's Word. Don't you think the devil knows this? So he hits you with everything he's got as you begin to take your first steps toward faith. Why? Because he knows that your faith coupled with action will get a response from God.

"Yea, a man will say, Thou hast faith, and I have works: show me thy faith without thy works, and I will show thee my faith by my works" (James 2:18).

HALF-TRUTHS ARE DEADLY

The devil was trying to steal my faith. You may ask, "How does the devil steal your faith?" Simply by challenging your most recent decision to obey God's Word. He accomplishes this by asking you questions laced with half-truth. What is a half-truth? Half-truth is inaccurate, leaving out or adding important details. This is exactly what he did with Eve. You see him entering the garden as a serpent and then he began to question her about God's recent instructions.

"...Yea, hath God said...? For God doth know that in the day ye eat thereof, then your eyes shall be opened, and ye shall be as gods, knowing good and evil."
Genesis 3:1;5

His questions are meant to cast a shadow of doubt concerning God's instructions to you. He's trying to get you to question God just enough to forfeit any actions toward faith! Look at this again:*"Hath God said?..."* Can you see him trying to cast doubt in the mind of Eve? It worked and Eve even responded with a half-truth of her own.

> *"...God hath said, Ye shall not eat of it, neither shall you touch it lest you die"* (Genesis 3:3).

God never told Eve not to *touch* the fruit...He only instructed her not to eat it. The devil will always use the Bible to question you, because his objective is to challenge God's Word. Faith requires the Word of God to survive...it's the foundation of faith. So he steals your faith through unbelief about what God really meant to say. Believe it or not, he knows the Bible better than any person alive today. Why wouldn't he know it? He was accustomed to being in the presence of God on a continual basis. However, when he questions you about what God said, he will always add or omit relevant information concerning the Bible. You must know the Word of God and look at it in its entirety.

PLEASE, LET ME KEEP MY *MICHELIN* TIRES

I was living high! Because my fiancee (who is now my wife) had just purchased four brand new Michelin tires for my 1987 Oldsmobile Calais. You might be thinking to yourself, "Excited, over tires?" That's right! They weren't just any tires...they were *Michelin.* You see, growing up around the Coontz home was tough financially. We didn't have much money. We were a typical lower middle-class family who were struggling to make ends meet. My father loved cars, although I never remember him owning a new one. My father said on numerous occasions, "Michelin is the best tire made; if you can afford them...buy them!" He never owned a set of Michelin tires while I was young; however, in later years he was able to afford them. So naturally one of my goals in life was to have a set of Michelin tires.

Less than 30 days after I purchased my Michelin tires I wrecked my car. I was now facing an incredible dilemma. My only transportation was now smashed and unable to be driven. I thought things were supposed to get better after I started giving. I was puzzled and didn't understand why God was allowing this to happen. A week later the insurance adjuster called me and said that it would cost too much to fix the car, so they totaled it. He also told me they would be unable to pay off my car completely because I owed too much on the note. I said to him, "You've got to be kidding me!" He assured me that they were serious. Just when I thought it couldn't get any worse! I told him that I had just purchased four new Michelin tires and asked if I could get them off of the car. He responded with, "No, but I can sell them to you." I thought to myself, "Sell them to me — I've already bought them once!" You don't have to be a genius to figure out what I told him. I now had no car, and my Michelin tires were gone too. How could my financial life be crumbling around me so quickly? I was disgusted about everything! Yet, strange as it may seem, my faith seemed to remain strong. I once again reaffirmed my commitment to God and declared for the second time, *"I'm still tithing and giving no matter what happens!"*

About a week passed when I received a phone call from the bank. They said I still had an outstanding balance of $2000, and they wanted to know how I was planning to pay this off. Good question! I had no idea how I was going to pay off a $2000 debt without any way of getting to work. My credit was ruined, and even if it weren't I couldn't have qualified for a loan. However, I made arrangements to send them $100 each month until it was paid off.

Here is a valuable principle for financial success...pay your debts. Even though the bank had no collateral, morally I was obligated to pay them back. So I did. Many are facing financial struggles today because they refuse to honor their word. If you have made a financial commitment... then pay it. It is yet another step toward faith, and it gives God another opportunity to provide you with financial provision. God helped me not only to pay the bank off, I paid them off in less than a year and was never late with a payment. *Try it...it works!*

I *BROKE* THE BACK OF POVERTY WITH A $20 SEED

I broke the back of poverty with a $20 *seed* sown *consistently.* When I made my promise to God to start giving a portion of my income I was only making $200 each week. Every week I set aside ten percent of my money for God as my tithe. I consistently sowed $20, no matter what my financial condition looked like... faithfully...consistently...week after week...*I sowed.* God rewards obedience, faithfulness, and His Word!

I have just spent several pages telling you about my personal financial struggles. I have tried to illustrate through each circumstance the spiritual battle that took place in my life. Struggle came because I wanted to move beyond poverty into the realm of abundance. Of course, the devil wanted to keep me poor and broke. I refused! Consequently the battle began.

The area of money is very much a spiritual subject. God has a financial plan for your life, and its foundation is the Word of God. My financial poverty really existed because I refused to operate by faith in God's Word. Although I knew the scriptures concerning the subject of tithing and giving, yet I never operated by these principles because of fear. Fear kept me from releasing my money to God because I believed I would then have less. However, God's Word clearly says, *"Give and it shall be given unto you...."* I simply didn't believe this, because if I did, then I would have been giving. *It's really that simple.* I know that we try to make the subject of money as it relates to God's Word more complicated than it is. My struggles financially were birthed from my unwillingness to practice God's principles concerning giving. Again, it's that simple. Your financial harvest always begins with a *SEED!*

The Four Laws Of The Harvest...
You qualify for harvest by your seed sowing.

The laws of the harvest declare that before there can be a harvest a seed must be sown. You cannot expect a harvest without first sowing seed. Farmer Jones knows not to expect a harvest if he hasn't sown any seeds. He knows that his only hope for survival is in the life of the seed!

*"Give, and it shall be given unto you; **good** measure, **pressed** down, and **shaken** together, and **running over**, shall men give into your bosom. For with the same measure that ye mete withal it shall be measured to you again"* (Luke 6:38).

*"But remember this...if you **give** a little, you will reap a little. A farmer who **plants** a few seeds will get only a small crop, but if he plants much, he will reap much"* (2 Corinthians 9:6, TLB).

Law # 1....The Seed Must First Be Sown.

Every farmer knows that every seed has an invisible instruction and contains life. What is a seed? Anything that you can sow is a seed. Time is a seed. Kindness is a seed. Love is a seed. Money is a seed. Your life is a collection of seeds. Every seed has an invisible instruction that cannot be seen with the human eye. Your seed may be small. It may seem insufficient to meet your needs; however, your seed is alive and it contains an instruction to multiply and become more, and it's instructed to reproduce after its kind.

- You sow apple seeds to reap apples.
- You sow peach seeds to reap peaches.
- You sow tomato seeds to reap tomatoes.

You cannot see apples, peaches, or tomatoes when you sow the seeds. However, you recognize that because of the invisible life contained in the seed, when the seed is sown, over time the evidence of life will emerge and your harvest will flourish. *Everything Begins With A Seed!*

*"Be not deceived; God is not mocked: for whatsoever a man **soweth**, that shall he* also **reap.**"

Galatians 6:7

Anything within your reach can be considered a *seed.* God asked Moses..."What is in your hand?" The prophet said to the widow woman... "Bring me vessels, not a few." Jesus asked the lad..."What do you have to eat?"

• Moses had only a staff.
• The widow woman possessed a small amount of oil.
• The lad had only a few fishes and some bread.

Yet each of them possessed something within their reach...*and with God it was enough!* What do you have within your reach? It can be your seed. Never take inventory of what you don't have. If you do then you will never sow. Something right now...within your reach...it is enough...*Sow it!*

Law # 2...You Sow The Seed Into Good Ground.

It is just as important *where* you sow as it is *what* you sow. Every farmer spends time qualifying the soil. He wants to make sure that where he is sowing is good, fertile ground. He will spend extensive time cultivating the soil, getting it prepared for the seed. *Note: The seed needs the ground more than the ground needs the seed!* Make sure that the ground you're sowing into is fertile ground. You can determine if where you're sowing is fertile soil by asking yourself these questions: Is it Biblical? What does God's Word say about it? Has there been fruit in the past? Good ground always yields a bountiful harvest! Is there accountability both financially and spiritually? What does your inner voice of the Holy Spirit tell you? You should have an inner peace about what you're doing.

"And the **peace** *of God, which passeth all under-standing, shall keep your hearts and minds through Christ Jesus"* (Philippians 4:7).

Law # 3...You Sow The Seed To The Harvest.

What do I mean by sowing *to* the harvest? If a farmer has a bad year and his crop doesn't produce, the following year he doesn't sow less seed, he sows more seed to make up for the previous bad year. The farmer recognizes that he needs to make up for two years instead of one. He will do whatever he has to do to get more seeds, because he knows that he will never reap more from sowing less! You always sow your seed in direct proportion to how much harvest you're expecting to receive. *If you have big needs you must sow many seeds!*

Law # 4...You Sow In Faith And Wait Patiently.

What follows sowing? Reaping, right? *Wrong!* The Bible talks about seed time *then* harvest. *Seed...Time...Harvest.*

"While the earth remaineth, **seedtime** *and* **harvest,** *and cold and heat, and summer and winter, and day and night shall not cease"* (Genesis 8:22).

Waiting follows sowing. I have never seen a farmer yet sow one day and expect a harvest the next day. Have you? After you've sown your seed into fertile soil, you must wait patiently for your seed to germinate, take root, and eventually produce your harvest — seed...time...harvest. You must wrap your faith around your seed and believe what God said about the laws of sowing and reaping! *Faith Is Rejecting Our Five Senses And Embracing Hope!*

*"But without **faith** it is impossible to please him: for he that cometh to God must **believe** that he is, and that he is a **rewarder** of them that diligently seek him."*
Hebrews 11:6

PERPETUAL SEASON OF HARVEST

When you operate under these Four Laws of the Harvest you will place into motion what I call "momentum harvest." The momentum is similar to walking on a level escalator in an airport that carries you from one terminal to the other. As you walk the escalator moves too, the momentum builds up and your speed increases. You almost cover twice the ground in only half the time. God doesn't always want you sowing from your needs or "must have a miracle today" circumstances. He wants to move you into a place where you are sowing from abundance. There also is what I call "momentum sowing." This is when you sow from the harvest you're presently enjoying to reap from the harvest that follows the next cycle. *Your Seeds Of Today Create Your Harvest Of Tomorrow!* You are continually sowing so that you stay in a perpetual season of harvest. This is what the Bible calls...ABUNDANCE!

Nine *Biblical* Reasons Why We Need More Money.

Money is relative. Everyone requires a certain amount of money to survive — all of us can agree on this. *How much money is enough?* While all of us can offer our opinions concerning this question — how many of us have searched the scriptures? *I have.* **God Requires...**

1. Us To Tithe & Give Offerings. *"Will a man rob God? Yet ye have robbed me. But you say, Wherein have we robbed thee? In tithes and offerings"* (Malachi 3:8).

2. Us To Send The Gospel To The World. *"Go...teach all nations, baptizing them in the name of the Father, and of the Son, and of the Holy Ghost"* (Matthew 28:19).

3. Us To Provide For Our Families. *"...if any provide not for his own, and especially for those in his own house...he is worse than an infidel"* (1 Timothy 5:8).

4. Us To Help The Poor. *"He that hath pity upon the poor lendeth money to the Lord..."* (Proverbs 19:17).

5. Us To Lend To Every Believer Who Asks. *"Give to him that asketh thee, and from him that would borrow of thee turn not thou away"* (Matthew 5:42).

6. Us To Have Enough So We Don't Have To Borrow Money To Live. *"The rich ruleth over the poor, and the borrower is the servant to the lender"* (Proverbs 22:7).

7. Us To Save. *"Go to the ant, thou sluggard; consider her ways, and be wise"* (Proverbs 6:6).

8. Us To Pay Taxes. *"...Render therefore unto Caesar the things which are Caesar's..."* (Matthew 22:21).

9. Us To Leave An Inheritance. *"A good man leaveth an inheritance for his children, as well as his grandchildren"* (Proverbs 13:22).

Resting In God's Will While Celebrating His Ways

"Let us therefore fear, lest, a promise being left us of entering into his rest, any of you should seem to come short of it."

Hebrews 4:1

CHAPTER 9

*O*ver 400 hundred years had passed before God's mighty power was once again displayed to Israel. Historians call this time in Biblical history *the dark ages*. It was a sad and dreary time for the Israelites...God's chosen people. Years of bondage and torment under the oppressive hands of the Egyptians left this once mighty Israelite people defeated and discouraged! The bellowing cry of this chosen race rang throughout the land for over four centuries. Finally, after years of torment, pain, and slavery their cry entered heaven and into the ears of God.

*"Now therefore, behold, the **cry** of the children of Israel is come unto me: and I have also **seen** the oppression wherewith the Egyptians oppress them."*

Exodus 3:9

God always raises up a deliverer to break the back of oppression and bondage in your life. It takes years of preparation and training before this person is ready to answer God's call. Although it's a process of time, God is patient and longsuffering during the process. Israel waited an additional thirty years after God initially heard their cry before He sent Moses. Why? Because He was preparing Moses as their deliverer! Throughout the Bible God has anointed ordinary people to carry His message of redemption, deliverance, and restoration. For example:

⇨ Noah *delivered* his family from the flood to continue the seed of man (Gen. 8:1).

⇨ Abraham *restored* the promise of the Covenant (Gen. 12:1).

⇨ David *delivered* the Israelites from Goliath (1 Sam. 17:37).

⇨ Nehemiah *restored* Jerusalem (Neh.1:1).

⇨ Moses *delivered* the Israelites from the Egyptians (Gen. 3:10).

Today, our deliverer is Jesus. He has purchased us with His blood at Calvary. No matter what questions are lurking in your mind, He is the answer to all of them. However, God doesn't always answer your cries swiftly because there is a *process* of time... preparation... and work He must complete in you. During this process it may seem like God is unconcerned about your dilemma or crisis. Yet this couldn't be farther from the truth. It's easy to focus on your present circumstances and become preoccupied with questions of doubt, unbelief, and fear when you're struggling. Human nature wants quick solutions, rewards without effort, and the pleasures of sin void of consequences. Yet God is more interested in the process of becoming than the final destination of being. You can become so distracted with being, you fail to remember that *being* is a process of *becoming*. Remember that to become what He's called you to be takes time...patience...and work. *It's a process!*

GOD USES EVERY *EXPERIENCE* TO COMPLETE THE PROCESS

Struggle is a fact of life. But you don't have to surrender and give up when faced with it! Life will throw at you various types of struggle: *family... financial...physical...spiritual...or natural.* Although the burden may be heavy at times, you don't have to be crushed under the weight of it. One of God's tools for molding and making you into what He wants you to become is struggle. God doesn't schedule your stress, pain, hurt, or defeat; however, He will use each experience as an opportunity to complete His process in you. Take this book, for instance; it's the result of a process of learning and revelation, much of which has come through pain, hurt, and mistakes. Yet through every struggle and unfortunate happening in my life, God has used them to prepare me for today. Why? Because growth rarely ever occurs with the absence of struggle.

Consequently, because God requires growth, He recognizes that struggle is a necessary ingredient for growth. That's why He has already made provision in His promises to give you *rest*. With God's promises you can obtain a rest regardless of the difficulty or struggle you might be facing today. The storm can be around you; however, it doesn't have to be in you! You will learn the difference between God's ways and His works.

You'll also learn how you can apply God's promises to your difficulty and discover the rest that He promises to every believer. Even right now while you're facing perhaps your greatest struggle, God is at work in your life. You can learn to...*Rest In God's Will, While Celebrating His Ways!* Here are *four principles* that will help answer any questions you may have concerning how to find a place in God where you can truly *rest*.

Principle # 1: Remember, You're In Covenant With God.

*"And God heard their groaning, and **remembered his covenant** with Abraham, with Isaac, and with Jacob"* (Exodus 2:24).

A *covenant* is a formal, binding agreement between two parties to do or not to do something. Biblical covenants reflect God's sovereign declaration to establish a legal agreement between Himself and humanity. Many Biblical covenants are unconditional — God commits Himself to accomplish something regardless of whether or not humanity executes their part of the agreement. A Biblical covenant, however, usually contains promised blessings for those who obey the terms of the covenant and guarantees punishment for a refusal to comply. God is a covenant-making God! **Note:** There are eight major covenants found in the Bible. These covenants help us to understand God's unfolding plan to redeem humanity from the curse of sin and provide details about His kingdom on earth. The eight major covenants are:

#1...*The Edenic Covenant* (Gen. 2:15). This covenant is God's first with people. This covenant guarantees several rights and requirements for people.

#2...The Adamic Covenant (Gen. 3:15). This covenant stipulated the conditions under which sinful people must live until the redemption of the earth in the millennial kingdom of Christ.

#3...The Noahic Covenant (Gen. 9:8). God established this covenant to reconfirm the conditions of the Adamic covenant and to authorize human government as a control for violence.

#4...The Abrahamic Covenant (Gen. 15:4). This covenant declared God's sovereign choice to bless Israel and the nations through Abraham and his descendant, the Messiah.

#5...The Mosaic Covenant (Ex. 19:15). This covenant expanded the promises made to Abraham.

#6...The Palestinian Covenant (Deut. 30:1-10). This covenant described the divinely appointed conditions that God established for Israel's occupation of the Promised Land.

#7...The Davidic Covenant (2 Sam. 7:16). God made additional promises to Israel through this covenant.

#8...The New Covenant (Heb. 8:8-12). This is the last of the eight. It guarantees salvation based on God's promises to transform the hearts of His people. It also guarantees that all sin will be forgiven forever through Christ's atoning work on the cross.

Through covenants God establishes man's responsibility to obey a specific instruction from Him. God declares, *"I will...."* Man's obedience leads him to blessing, while disobedience leads him to discipline and chastisement. God's promises always come with an *"if."*

The Israelites' slavery was first predicted to Abram in a dream, while at the same time God promised their deliverance and return to the Promised Land.

*"...Thy seed shall be a **stranger** in a land that is not theirs, and shall **serve** them; and they shall **afflict** them four hundred years. And also that nation, whom they shall serve, will I judge: and afterward shall they come out with **great substance"** (Genesis 15:13,14).*

Why did God allow the Israelites to suffer slavery for over four centuries? Because it was foretold to Abram many years before in a dream. Why should we have faith in God's covenant promises? The reason is because of His character. God cannot lie!

*"**God is not a man, that he should lie**; neither the son of man, that he should repent: hath he said, and shall he not do it? or hath he spoken, and shall he not make it good?"* (Numbers 23:19).

THREE LAWS UPHOLDING THE CHARACTER OF GOD

1. The Law of Integrity — *God Will Not Break One Law To Fulfill Another Law.*

*"In hope of eternal life, which **God, that cannot lie,** promised before the world began"* (Titus 1:2).

Think of the one person that you know today that you'll trust with your life. Assume that person climbed the Empire State Building and leaped off without a parachute. What do you suppose would happen? You're right. He would become scrambled eggs after he collided with the cement below. No matter how good your friend may have been, or how honest, kind, and generous his life...he would die. Why? Because the law of gravity says so.

God's integrity will not allow Him to break any of His laws to fulfill another one of His laws. This is comforting to me because I know that if I follow His laws then He is obligated to fulfill them. How do I know this? Because He *cannot lie*, and His character will not allow Him to!

2. The Law of Respect — *God Gives Everyone The Same Opportunity To Obey.*

> *"For there is no **respect** of persons with God."*
> Romans 2:11

Did you know that God has favorites? *That's right!* This law is the most misunderstood of all His laws. Why? Because most don't understand the real meaning of *"is no respect of persons."* This simply means that God has given everyone the same opportunity to obey His instructions. The following verses further explain this point.

> *"Who will **render** to every man **according** to his deeds"* (Romans 2:6).

> *"But glory, honor, and peace, to every man that **worketh good**..."* (Romans 2:10).

Your deeds will determine God's response to you. If you do good things then you will reap peace; however, bad things will produce evil results. God will not give one person an opportunity that He will not give another. Everyone has equal opportunity to obey God. Yet God is more pleased with the obedient listener than He is with the rebel. Thus, He prefers the obedient over the disobedient. Are you one of God's favorites?

3. The Law of Reciprocity--*God Will Punish Or Reward Every Action Taken.*

*"Be not deceived; God is not mocked: whatsoever a man soweth, that shall **he also reap**."*

Galatians 6:7

God's kingdom both on earth and in heaven is a system governed by laws and principles. God's character upholds every word spoken by Himself and every promise that was uttered from His lips. This system promises to reward the obedient, while punishing the disobedient. Newton's Law, which originates from God's system, says: For every action there is an equal action. *God's Law:* Whatsoever you soweth, you shall reap! "Whatsoever" means anything you sow... good or bad. It may seem like some are getting away with wrongdoing. You may even think that God has forgotten your labor of love. God *sees.* He *knows.* He will *repay.* God is not mocked! This law provides the confidence of knowing that everything He promised to Abraham, Isaac, and Jacob has been promised to you. Why? His covenant and God's character upholds His Word! The Israelites suffered for over four hundred years before God acknowledged hearing their groaning. He then remembered the covenant He established with Abraham, Isaac, and Jacob. Remember, you're in covenant with God too!

Principle # 2: Discern The Difference Between God's Works And His Ways.

*"And I am sure that the king of Egypt will not let you go, no, not by a **mighty hand**"* (Exodus 3:19).

*"...I will stretch out my hand, and smite Egypt with all my **wonders**..."* (Exodus 3:20).

God stretched forth His hand performing many spectacular works. Yet each time the king of Egypt became more calloused and obdurate toward Him. Why? Because God's works are different than His ways. For example, after the Israelites exited Egypt, God displayed a parade of His mighty works. The first was when they crossed the Red Sea. Afterward, they traveled for miles looking for water. They eventually approached Marah hoping to find water there; however, the water was bitter. Less than three days after the Israelites witnessed the parting of the Red Sea they began to murmur against God. *"Would to God we had died by the hand of the Lord in Egypt...."* God heard them and showed Moses a tree and instructed him to cast it into the water; immediately the water became sweet. God also led them by a cloud during the daytime and a pillar of fire by night. He provided them with fresh bread each morning via shuttled by quail airlines. They saw water come from a rock. Even their clothes and shoes lasted for over forty years. God displayed His power through a variety of works. Nearly one million Israelites witnessed these works both in Egypt and in the wilderness, yet they returned their thanks by murmuring against God in unbelief! Why? Because you rarely ever learn from God's works...you only learn about Him from His ways!

➤ God's works display His power
➤ God's ways reveal Him
➤ God's works expose *His* heart
➤ God's ways expose *your* heart
➤ God's works declare to humanity His existence
➤ God's ways express Himself to humanity through you
➤ God's works impart His *miracles* to humanity
➤ God's ways pour *Himself* in you

The Israelites wandered in the wilderness for forty years because of their unbelief. Why? Because they saw His works, and yet never really knew His ways. Allow God to work in you!

Principle # 3: Discover God's Will For Your Life.

*"Jesus saith unto them, My meat is to do the **will** of him that sent me, and to **finish** his works"* (John 4:34).

Once you've discovered the difference between God's works versus His ways the only question remaining is *"How do I discover the will of God for my life?"* First of all, God's will for your life was never intended to become a mystery to you. Although some try to make it more difficult than it really is, it has always been God's heart to reveal Himself to you in various ways. Yet many become confused and disillusioned about God's will because they've been taught they should wander in the wilderness of life just like the Israelites did. **Note:** They wandered around in circles within a forty mile radius because of their unbelief. It was never God's will for them to wander; His plan originally called for a direct entrance into Canaan.

Neither is it God's will for you to wander or become confused about His will for your life. Here are three keys to discovering God's will for you.

Key # 1...His Will Is Revealed Through The Bible.

*"**Study** to show thyself approved unto God, a workman that needeth not to be ashamed, rightly dividing **the word of truth**"* (2 Timothy 2:15).

One of the most amazing facts about the Bible is its endurance through the ages. It's one of the oldest books in the world; sections of it were written more than 25 centuries ago. God's will for your life will first be revealed to you through His Word. Although it happened many years ago I still remember the day when I was confronted by a co-worker of mine. I was working in a grocery store while I was still in high school. It was a habit for me to discuss the Bible with some of them who were searching for answers. One day while I was working in the meat section, Chris came over to me with a smile on his face and declared, "Todd, I've found where the Bible contradicts itself." I answered him, "Where?" He began to chronicle the events that led him to that conclusion while endeavoring to prove the inaccuracy of the Bible. After listening to him for a moment I discovered that he had taken the Bible out of context, pulling scriptures indiscriminately from one passage to another. In just a few minutes I showed him within the context of scripture where his original conclusion was wrong. He conceded. I then said to him, *"Chris, the Bible only contradicts the sin you're presently committing."* He looked at me and walked away.

God's will for your life will unfold as you study His written Word. *Read* the Bible. *Study* it entirely. *Memorize* a scripture a day. You will discover that His Word will come alive in your life as His will unfolds. *God Will Use His Word As The Instrument For Revealing His Will!*

Key # 2...His Will Is Revealed Through People.

*"And at the **mouth of two witnesses,** or **three witnesses,** shall he that is worthy of death be put to death; but at the mouth of one witness he shall not be put to death"* (Deuteronomy 17:6).

Another tool that God uses to reveal His will in your life is people. Various people will enter and exit your life. Some will remain, becoming a trusted friend or teacher. Others will abandon you, forgetting any involvement they may have had in your past. Yet God uses people to confirm His will for your life according to His Word. You must discern the difference between those who are sent by God to help you and those who have been sent by the devil to destroy you. How can you tell the difference? First of all, look at their past decisions they made for themselves. You want good decision makers guiding the choices you have to make. Secondly, do they really care about your success? Or are you only somebody whom they're using to advance their selfish agenda? *You must discern this.* Finally, do they know what they're talking about? Have they been where you want to go? You don't ask a 400 lb. person how to lose weight. Ask questions from those qualified to offer solutions. Surround yourself with a "circle of council." Use this criteria to qualify them along with what the Bible tells you. *I have.*

Key # 3...His Will Is Revealed By The Holy Spirit.

*"But God hath **revealed them** unto us **by his Spirit**: for the Spirit searcheth all things, yea, the deep things of God."* (1 Corinthians 2:10).

Have you ever been around somebody who acts mystical concerning the Holy Spirit? They leave the impression that we're not supposed to know "spiritual things." Or worse, they over-spiritualize everything! They make statements like "Oh, it's much too deep for your natural mind" or "You will only know after you've fasted for forty days." Sound familiar? In addition to their quirky way of approaching "spiritual things" they will even quote the Bible. One of the most misunderstood verses in the whole Bible is in Isaiah.

*"For **my thoughts** are not your thoughts, neither are **my ways** your ways, saith the Lord"* (Isaiah 55:8).

Anytime something happens that seems to be without any plausible answer or an acceptable solution, this verse gets quoted. Really, this passage isn't putting the emphasis on God's thoughts or His ways, but rather the responsibility is placed on you. What do I mean by this? God requires you to bring your thinking to a higher level and to negate your ways for His ways, acknowledging that He thinks much higher thoughts than you do and that His ways are superior to yours. This scripture is intended to bring you to a place of obedience. You are to exchange your thoughts and ways for His. The Bible makes it very clear that the "spiritual things" of God are not a mystery. In fact, it's really just the opposite. A good argument can be made that by not knowing the "spiritual things" you could be considered lazy. Why? Because it takes effort to search the scriptures for answers, to pray until peace comes, and to believe God in spite of a crisis. *Knowing The Will of God Requires Diligence!*

Why? God Requires You To *Know* "Spiritual Things"

> *"Now we have received, not the spirit of the world, but the Spirit which is of God; that **we might know the things** that are freely given to us by God."*
>
> 1 Corinthians 2:12

God's will is revealed to you through the Spirit. Why? So you may know the things that He freely gives to you. Paul, the writer of Corinthians, makes it clear that God requires you to know His will so you can be the recipient of all that He has to give you.

Principle # 4: Learn To Rest While Facing Struggles.

> *"Lay not wait, O wicked man, against the dwelling of the righteous; **spoil not his resting place:** For a just man falleth seven times and **riseth up again**: but the wicked shall fall into mischief."* (Proverbs 24:15-16).

When was the last time you had a good night's sleep? I mean you slept all night long and when morning arrived you felt *rested*. For many this is a fantasy. I'm told that hospitals have more reported cases of sleep deprivation than at any other time in history. Many have been diagnosed with insomnia, which is a sleeping disorder. The average person to-day gets less than six hours of sleep each night, while studies suggest that the average person really requires eight hours to function normally. If you haven't already figured it out, a lack of sleep is a real problem facing most people today. Yet, al-though God has provided His children with the promise of rest, many who proclaim Jesus as their Savior candidly admit they too have trouble sleeping. Why? I believe that it's a culmina-tion of several things.

- Long hours at work
- Scheduling too many things in a day
- Improper diet
- A sporadic sleeping schedule
- Financial worry or family problems

These are some of the causes of *sleep deprivation.* I know that you haven't purchased this book to learn about all the causes; you're looking for real solutions. Many today are lack-ing sleep because of stress...anxiety...and fear. I want to share with you four keys that I've learned to depend on during times of struggle and setbacks in my life.

Key # 1...Evaluate Your Present Circumstances.

Sit down and document the problem you're facing. It's impor-tant to know what you're up against. If your problem is financial...then write down what you owe, listing them one by one. Then calculate how much you've been spending and what you've been spending your money on. Maybe it's a family prob-lem. Then schedule a meeting with that person and ask them what you can do to repair and restore the relationship. It could be a lack of money. Then take a look at your present skills and see what you can do to become more qualified to earn more money. I have only named a few possible sleep robbers. However, I know that there are many more. Whatever problems you may be facing today or struggle you're going through, it's important to evaluate your present circumstances. Then determine your course of action!

Key # 2... What's The Worst That Could Happen?

Did you know that *ninety percent* of what you worry about you can't do anything about? Yet you will lose valuable sleep worrying all night long about something you know you're incapable of changing, allowing it to rob you of the energy necessary to accomplish your task. Why? Because of the fear of something that can't be seen. Your mind was created to function in two ways: First...*Memory.* Second...*Imagination.* You can free up your mind for imagination by simply writing down things you need to remember. Your imagination is the creative part of your brain designed to function as a *"dreamer."* However, if your mind is given a diet of negative, fearful, and pessimistic happenings, it will react in a negative way. For example: Turn off the lights in a room and see how your mind will begin to conjure up a fearful imagination. Many have failed to recognize that they're not afraid "of the dark"; they're afraid of what could be "in the dark." How? Because the imagination of the mind says so.

I was recently discussing the past of my Pastor, Cesar Brooks (also a mentor and good friend) with him probing to find out how he was able to come back from incredible setbacks in his life. Cesar knows something about struggle! He told me that as a child he attended twenty-six schools before he graduated. He had five step-father's and lived in more than twenty-five different homes. He explained to me that he's been flat broke at least eight times, having to start all over again. I said to him, "How did you make it?" He told me that one of the things he would do to assure himself that he would make it was ask himself this question, *"What's the worst that could happen?"* This *key* brings your imagination into captivity!

It was November 26, 2000, when I received the news that my father had passed away. We were on our way home from spending Thanksgiving with him and my family. Just the night before we were laughing and having fun together. One day later my father and friend was dead. After receiving the news we immediately turned around and headed back home. While driving home my mind carried me back to the most memorable times spent with him. The early mornings when just he and I sat together drinking a cup of coffee. When he helped me change the oil in my car or put on new brakes. Cold winter mornings when he would fix me breakfast before we would start off on our hunting trip together. The phone calls I received every Sunday morning catching up on a week's news. Times too numerous to name...good times...times I really miss. My father was the bravest man I've ever known. He wasn't brave because of the absence of fear, but because he forged ahead despite his fears! I learned many valuable lessons from him. The greatest, perhaps, is this one. I remember him telling me one day, *"Todd, you have to face your fears head on; if you don't, they will conquer you."* My father was a retired Navy veteran who served his country proudly and with honor. He knew something about fear, but he also possessed courage. He faced most of his fears head on! That's why when I returned home to be with my mother, that night I slept on the bed where my father had died just that morning. It was the hardest thing I've ever done! I cried for about two hours thinking about how much I would miss him, while in my mind I could hear him saying, *"Todd, you have to face your fears head on."* So I did. That night I conquered the fear of loss and God helped me to fall asleep as I rested in His arms. I slept all night long.

Key # 3...Create A Plan For Your Success.

Y ou will be amazed at the things you can think of by simply committing it to paper. God always offers more than one solution; however, you want the best one for your particular circumstance. Writing helps you accomplish this. Ask God to help you create a plan that will help you move forward. *He will.*

Key # 4...Change Several Small Things.

I remember watching a movie one time with a man who had an incredible mental problem. His doctor recommended that instead of tackling the "big stuff" he should concentrate on taking "baby steps." One small step at a time. Small hinges swing big doors. A tiny key unlocks a huge vault. *Several Small Changes Can Create A Big Difference!*

Apply each of these principles and keys to your life and you will find yourself...*Resting In God's Will, While Celebrating His Ways.*

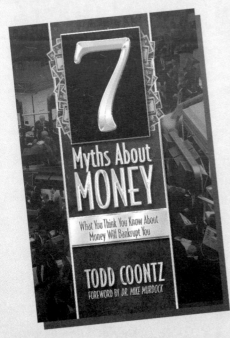

~ *For Further Information* ~

For additional copies of this book, for further information,
or for Todd Coontz's speaking schedule, please write or call:

ROCKWEALTH MINISTRIES
P.O. Box 6177
Aiken, SC 29804-6277

(803) 644-3271

Website:
www.toddcoontz.com